TELFORD
& EAST SHROPSHIRE

Admaston	3	Madeley	21
Albrighton	29	Malinslee	16
Arleston	10	Market Drayton	27
Bridgnorth	25	Muxton	7
Brookside	21	Newport	24
Broseley	23	Oakengates	12
Cleobury Mortimer	29	Priorslee	13
Coalbrookdale	19	Randlay	17
Dawley	16	Shawbirch	4
Donnington	6	Sheriffhales	14
Donnington Wood	13	Shifnal	18
Doseley	15	Snedshill	12
Hadley	11	St. George's	12
Hadley Castle	5	Stafford Park	17
Halesfield	22	Stirchley	16
Haybridge	10	Sutton Hill	21
Haygate	9	Telford Town Centre	1/2
Hortonwood	5	Trench	6
Ironbridge	23	Wellington	10
Ketley	11	Wombridge	12
Leegomery	4	Woodside	20
Lilleshall	8	Wrockwardine	9
Little Wenlock	19	Wrockwardine Wood	12

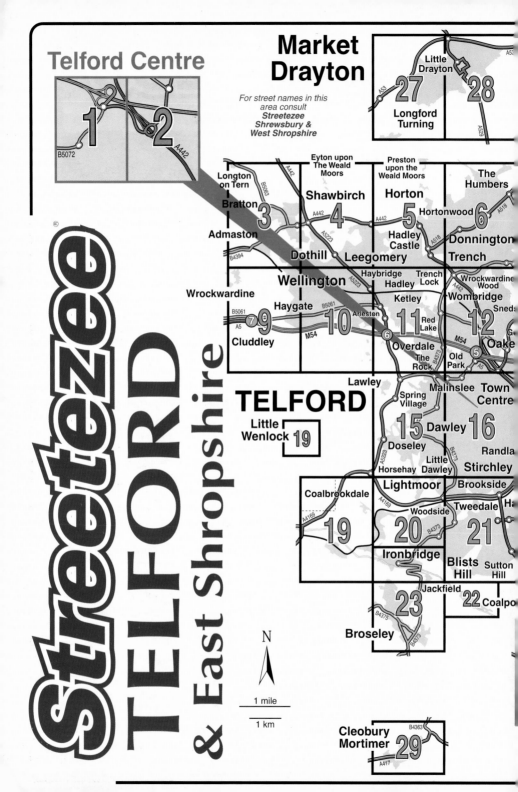

For street names in this area consult *Streetezee Stafford, Stone & Rugeley*

8

Lilleshall

24

Church Aston

Newport

uxton

8

Sheriffhales

ngton od

Hill

3 A5

14 A5

14

B4379

Priorslee

M54

4

Haughton

Shifnal

The Wyke

18

7

Kemberton

29

Albrighton

The Hobbins

5

26

ridgnorth

For street names in this area consult *Streetezee Kidderminster, Redditch & Bromsgrove*

Key to street plans

Street plans drawn at a scale of 4 inches to 1 mile

M4	Motorway
A48	A road (Trunk road)
B4281	B road
	Through road
	Dual carriageway
- - - - - -	Track
....	Footpath
	Railway/Station
	Built up area
	Recreation ground
	Woods and forest
H A&E	Hospital/A&E Dept.
✚	Health centre
	Petrol station
⊙ † ✡	Places of worship
◮	Police station
✉	Post Office
℄	Telephone
T	Toilet facility
P	Car parks (major)
🚐 ⛺	Caravan/camp site
i	Information centre
⊼	Picnic site
⛳	Golf course
M 📖	Museum/Library
🍺 🏨	Public house/Hotel
🎭	Theatre
▲ YHA	Youth Hostel
41 42 43	House numbers

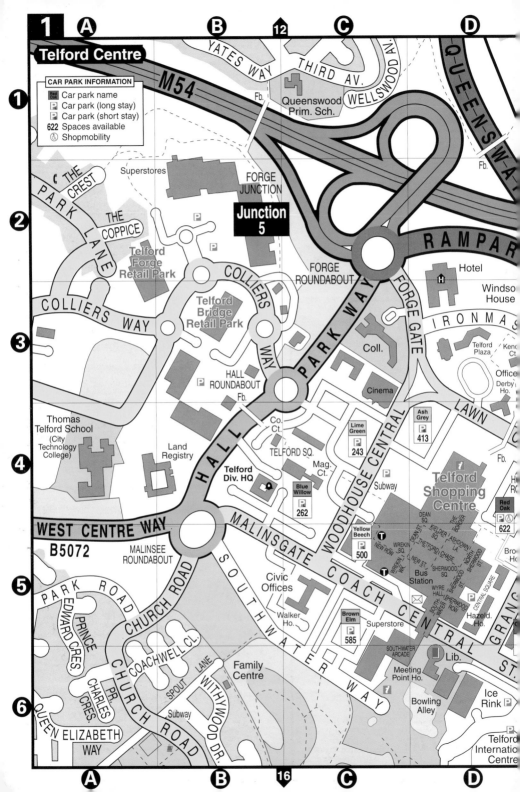

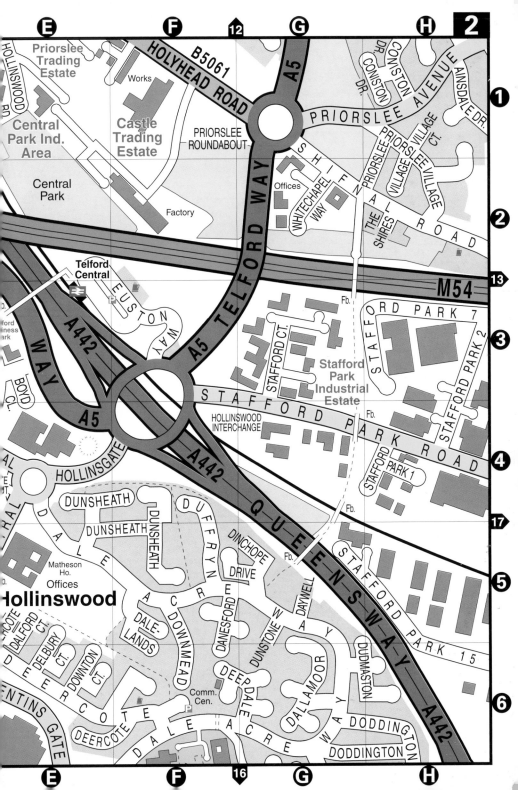

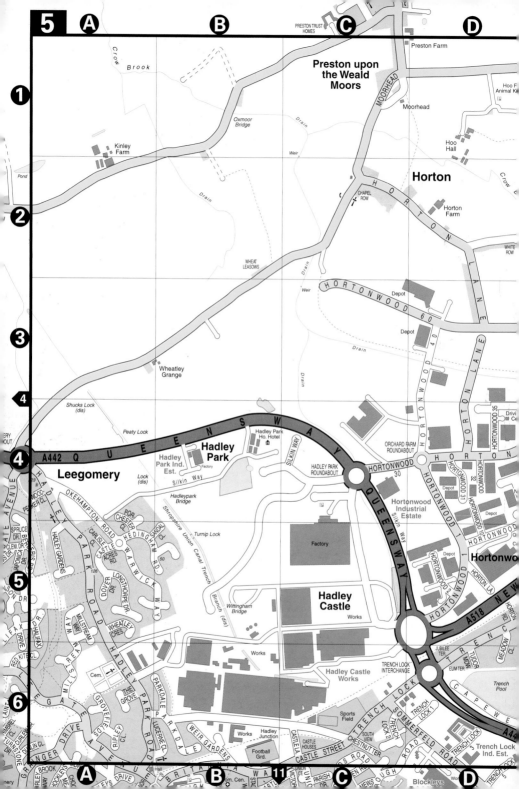

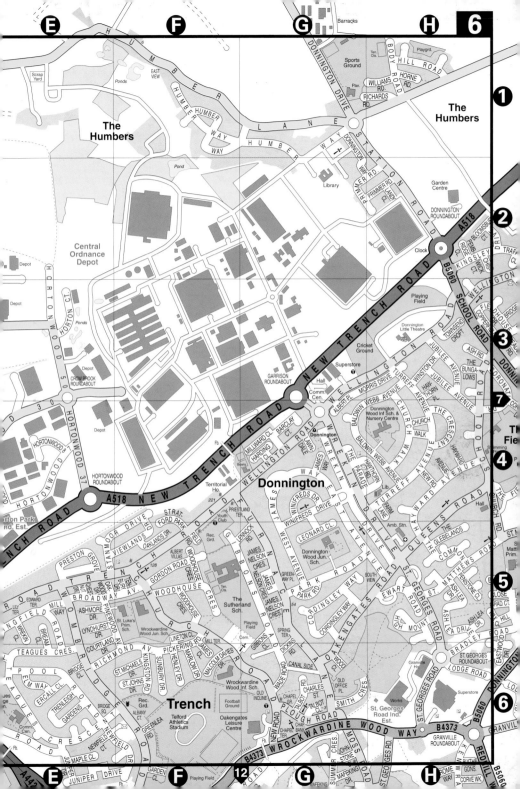

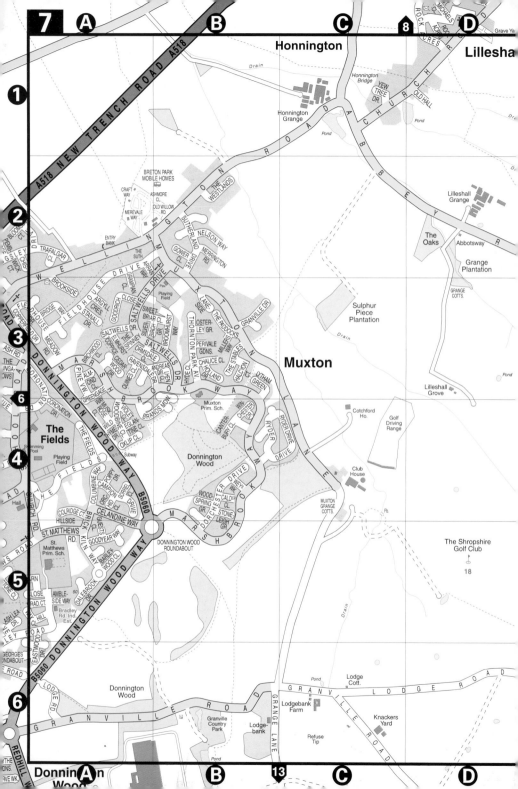

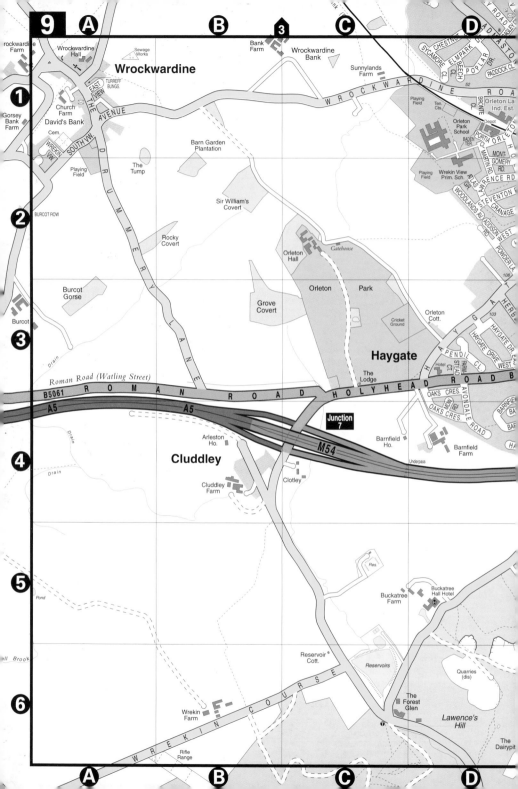

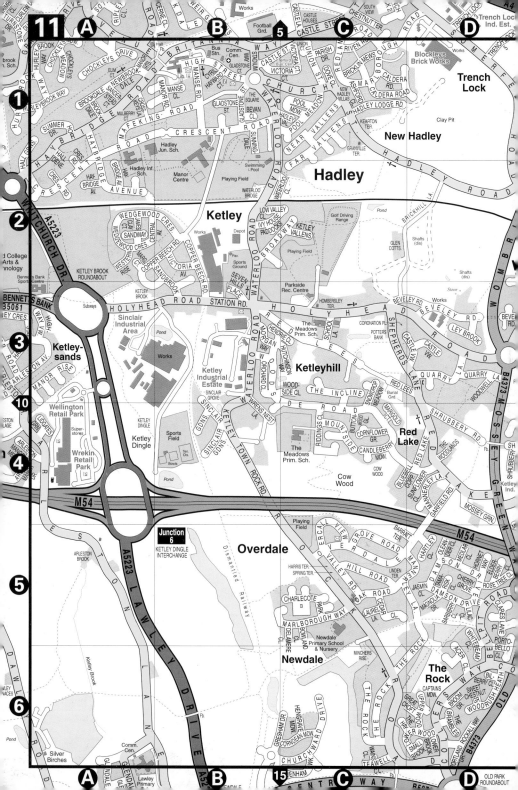

Cooper's
Coppice

Far
Wood

① Sheriffhales

Village
Farm

KETTLEMORE LANE

B4379

THE CRES. · SHAW · CROFT · LARKRISE FIELD · JAMES CL.

HALES
CT.

PINFOLD

Sheriffhales

Pond

Sheriffhales
Manor

MANOR
COTTS.

CHURCH LANE

THE
EVER-
GREENS

Playing
Field

Redhill
Farm

Pond

Pond

SHERIFFHALES DRIVE

Pond

② THE ROCK · MARSH ROAD

Vicarage

Sheriffhales
Prim. Sch.

Sluice

Drain

Sutherland
Ho.

B4379

Garage

27

③ A5 · **W A T L I N G   S T R E E T** · **A5**

Woodgreen

Ponds

Haughtonhill
Farm

④

Decker Hill
Farm

⑤

B4379

DECKER
HILL

Ponds

Club
House

Haughtonhill

Shifnal Golf Club

18

NEWPORT ROAD

stland-
brook
Cott.

Pond

⑥

B4379

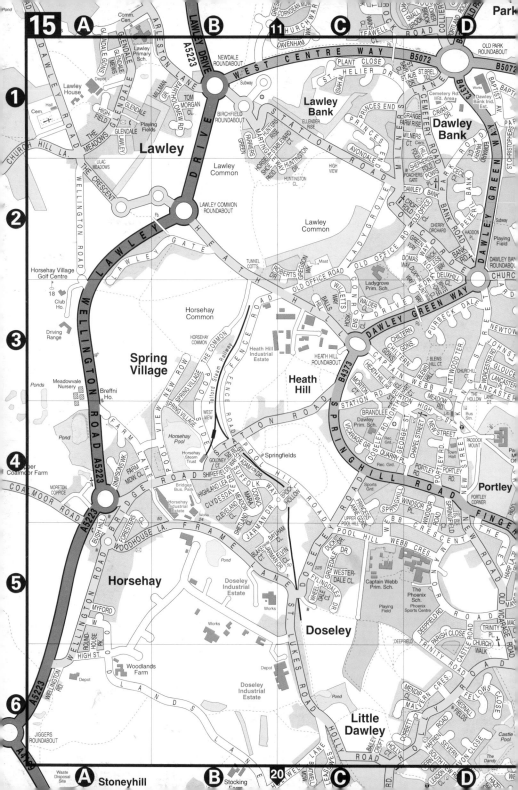

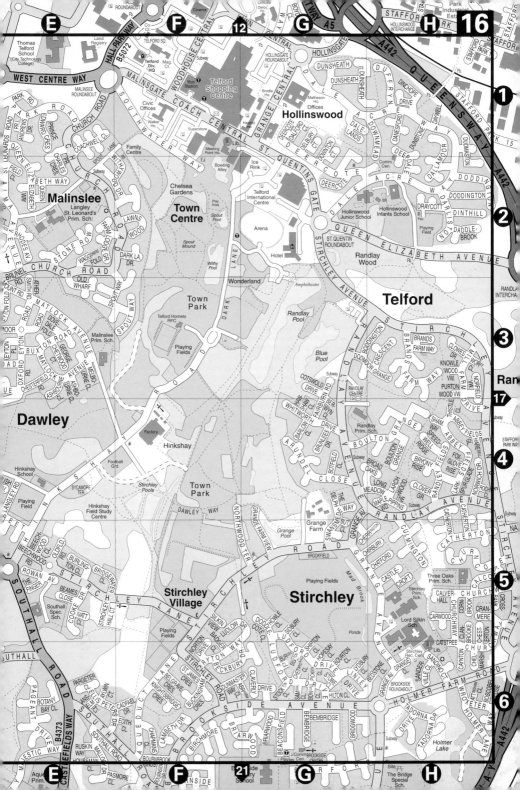

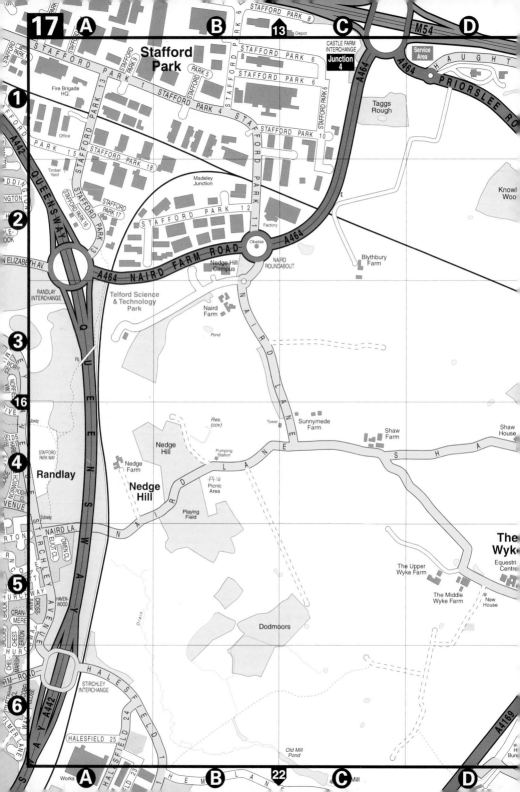

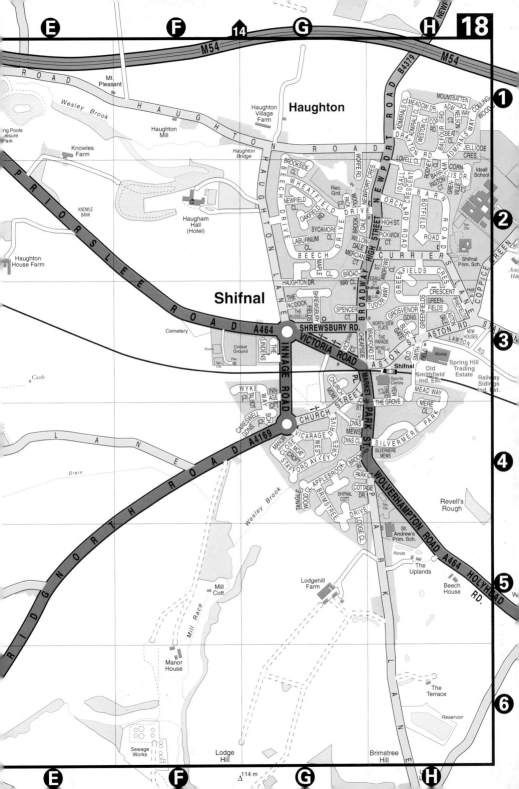

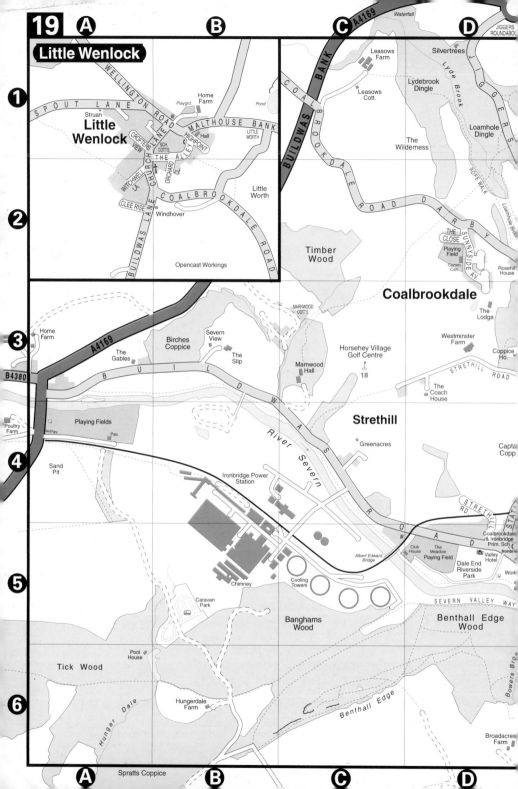

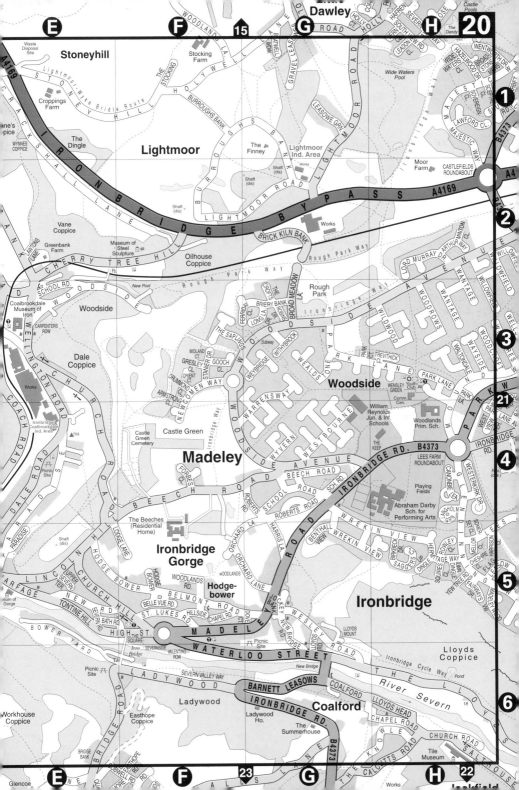

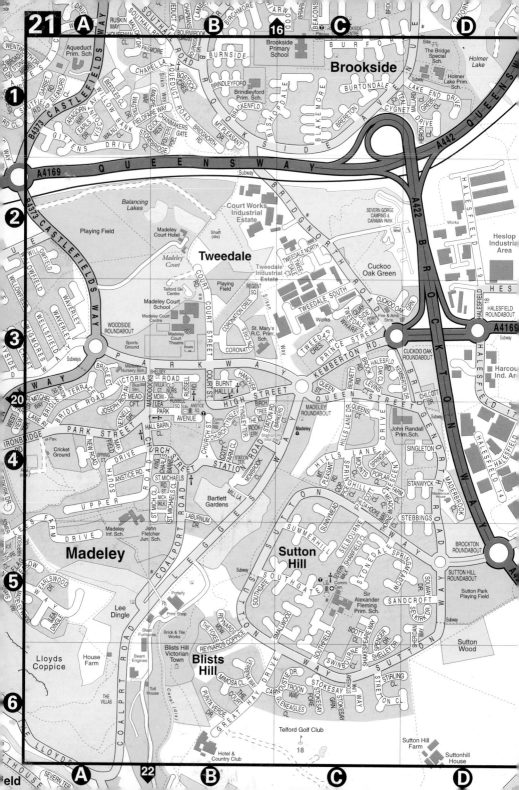

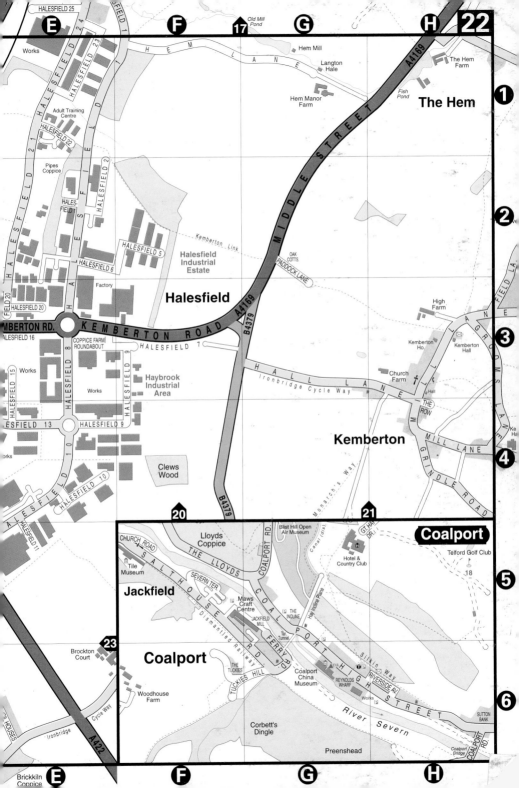

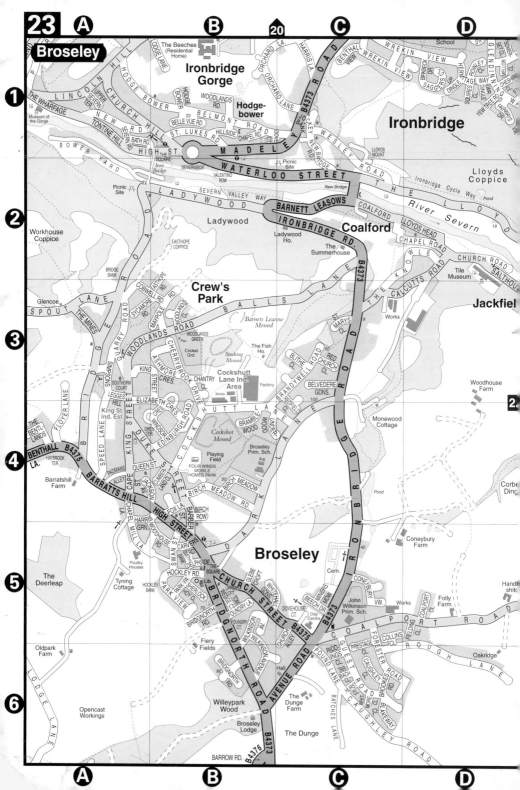

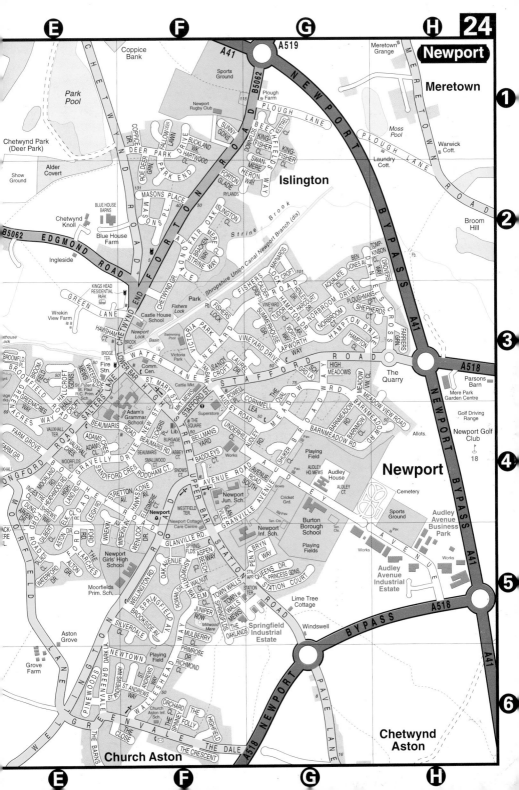

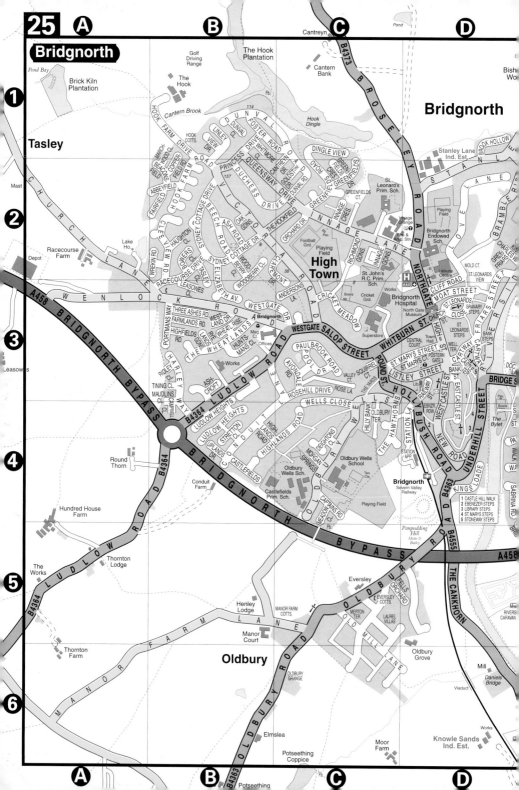

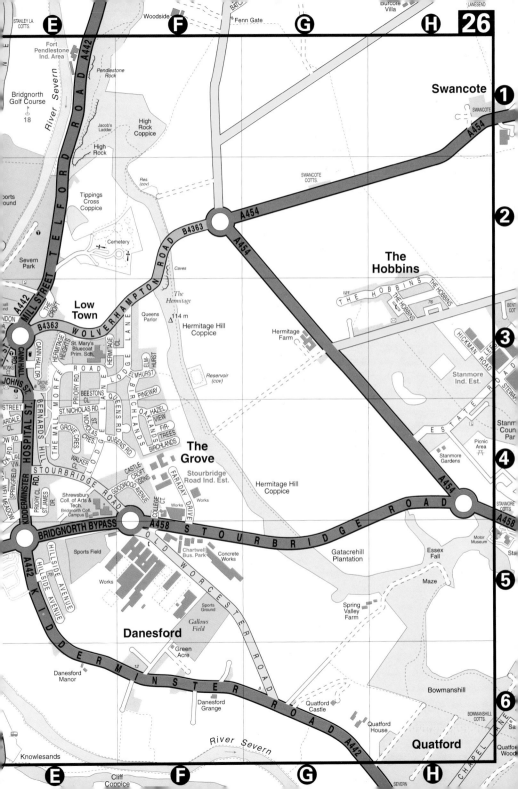

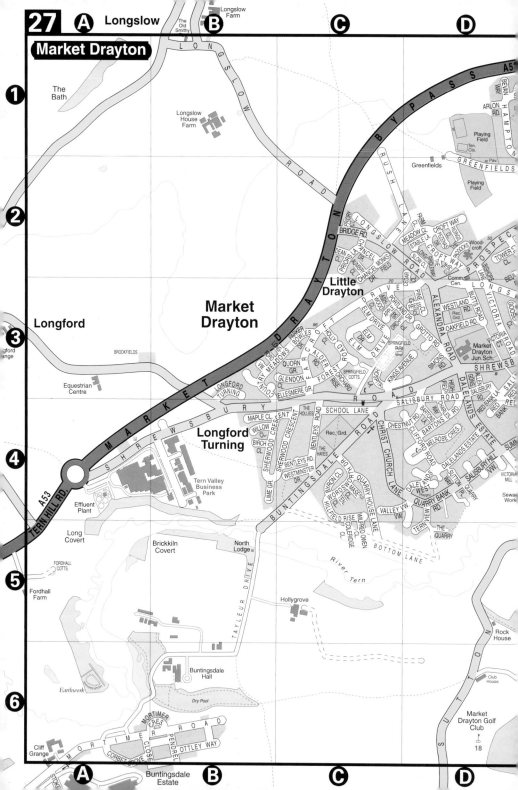

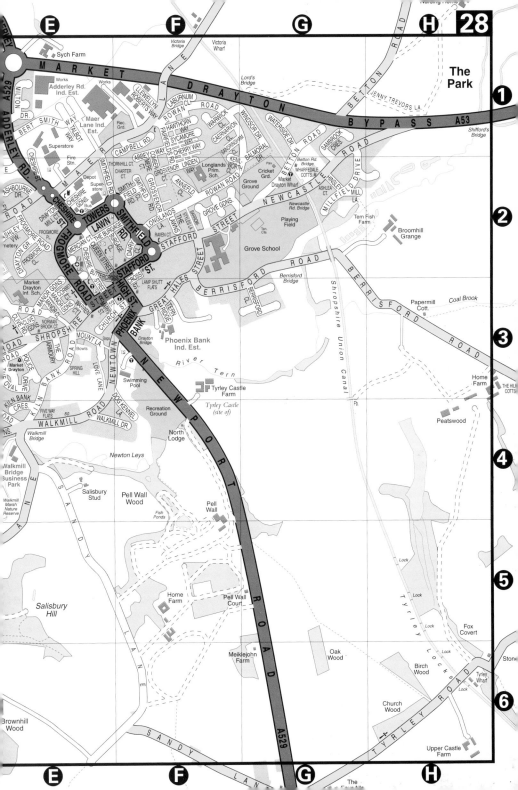

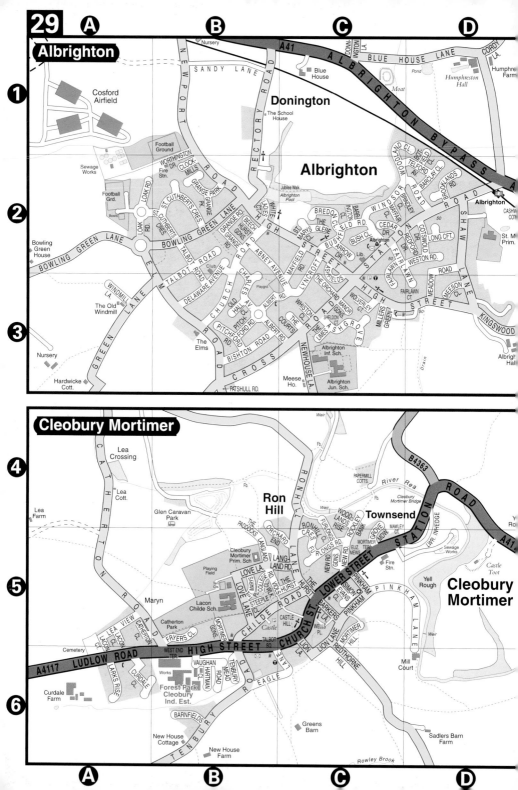

INDEX Abbreviations used

Allot(s).	Allotment(s)	Coll.	College	Fld(s).	Field(s)	Inf.	Infant	Off(s).	Office(s)	S.	South
Amb.	Ambulance	Comm.	Community	Flts.	Flats	Junc.	Junction	Orch(s).	Orchard(s)	Sq.	Square
App.	Approach	Comp.	Comprehensive	Fb(s).	Footbridge(s)	Jun.	Junior	Par.	Parade	Stn.	Station
Arc.	Arcade	Cov.	Covered	Gdns.	Gardens	La.	Lane	Pk.	Park	St.	Street
Av.	Avenue	Crn.	Corner	Gt.	Great	Lib.	Library	Pass.	Passage	Ten.	Tennis
Br.	Bridge	Cott(s).	Cottage(s)	Gra.	Grange	Lit.	Little	Pav.	Pavilion	Ter.	Terrace
Brd.	Broad	Cres.	Crescent	Grn.	Green	Lwr.	Lower	Pl.	Place	Up.	Upper
Bldg(s).	Building(s)	Cft.	Croft	Grd.	Ground	Mkt.	Market	Pr.	Precinct	Vic.	Vicarage
Bung(s).	Bungalow(s)	Ct.	Court	Gr.	Grove	Mag.	Magistrates	Prim.	Primary	Vw.	View
Bus.	Business	Dis.	Disused	Hd.	Head	Mdw(s).	Meadow(s)	Rec.	Recreation	Vlls.	Villas
Cara.	Caravan	Dr.	Drive	Hts.	Heights	Mem.	Memorial	Res.	Reservoir	Wk.	Walk
Cem.	Cemetery	E.	East	Hosp.	Hospital	Mon.	Monument	Resid.	Residential	Wy.	Way
Cen.	Centre	Ent.	Enterprise	Ho.	House	Mt.	Mount	Rd.	Road	W.	West
Cl.	Close	Est.	Estate	Ind.	Industrial	N.	North	Sch.	School	Yd.	Yard

Use of this Index: An alphabetical order is followed.

1. Each street name is followed by a map reference giving a page number and coordinates: Abbey Court **24** F4.

2. Names not appearing on the map are shown with an * and the reference of the nearest adjoining street:
Badhan Court*, Stadium Way **11** B1.

3. Where a street name appears more than once the reference is given: Castle Street **5** C6/**11** B1.

4. There is insufficient space to name all streets in situ, these appear in numbered lists and the reference is given:
Ebenezer Steps (2) **25** D4.

5. House numbers along streets are shown: *250.*

Locality Abbreviations:

Cleobury Mortimer	Cleo. Mort.	Jackfield	Jackfld.	Sheriffhales	Sheriff.
Coalbrookdale	Coalbrkdale.	Little Wenlock	Lit. Wen.	Wrockwardine	Wrkwdine.
Donnington Wood	Donn. Wd.	Market Drayton	Mkt. Dray.	Wrockwardine Wood	Wrkwdine. Wd.

A

Abbey Court **24** F4
Abbey Fields **16** H4
Abbey Road (Arleston) **10** G4
Abbey Road (Lilleshall)
........................**7** C1/**8** F6
Abbey Walls **12** E2
Abbey Way **28** F1
Abbeyfield **25** B2
Abbots Close **12** E2
Abbots Way **25** D2
Abdon Court **12** E2
Abelia Way **13** B4
Abney Avenue **29** B2
Abraham Close **16** F6
Acacia Drive **10** H1
Acer Close **11** D6
Acorn Mews **3** D4
Acorn Way **3** D4
Adams Close **24** E4
Adams Crescent **24** E4
Adamson Drive **15** B4
Adderley Road **28** E1
Addison Road **9** D2
Admaston Road **3** D6
Admaston Spa **3** C5
Admirals Close **18** H1
Admirals Way **18** H1
Ainsdale Drive **2** H1
Aintree Close **4** H6
Albacore Road **4** H5
Albany Court **6** F6
Albert Place **6** G4
Albert Road (Albrighton) **29** B3

Albert Road (Wellington) **10** F1
Albert Street **12** H3
Albert Villas **6** F5
Albion Street....................**12** G3
Albrighton Bypass............**29** C1
Alder Mead Close **3** C4
Alder Road **27** C3
Alderslee Close................**13** A4
Aldridge Close **13** B5
Alexandra Road (Mkt. Dray.)
....................................**27** D3
Alexandra Road (Wellington)
....................................**10** E2
Allcot Court*, Maurice Lee Av.
....................................**12** E2
Allen Gardens **27** D3
Allertons Meadow **3** C3
Alley, The **19** B2
Alma Avenue **16** E2
Alma Fields **16** E2
Almond Close **7** A3
Alton Grove **24** E5
Alverley Close **10** F1
Ambleside Way **7** A5
Ambry Close **27** C2
Andersons Lane **25** C3
Andreas Drive **7** B3
Annefield Close **28** F2
Anselm Court **16** E6
Anson Drive **4** H5
Anstice Road **21** A4
Anstice Square **21** B4
Apley Avenue **4** F6
Apley Castle **4** F5
Apley Cottages **4** G4

Apley Court **4** E4
Apley Drive **4** F6
Apple Grove **27** C3
Applebrook **18** G4
Appledore Gardens..........**10** E3
Aqualate Close **24** G3
Aqueduct Lane **16** F6
Aqueduct Road **21** B1
Aragorn Way **21** A1
Aralia Close **13** B4
Arches, The*, Park Street ..**10** F1
Arden Avenue **15** D3
Argyll Crescent **7** A3
Arleston Avenue **10** H3
Arleston Brook **11** A5
Arleston Court..................**10** H3
Arleston Hill......................**10** H5
Arleston Lane **10** H3/**11** A4/**15** B1
Arleston Manor Drive **10** H4
Arleston Manor Mews.......**10** H4
Arleston Village................**10** H4
Arlon Road **27** D1
Armoury Flats*, The Armoury
....................................**28** E3
Armoury, The **28** E3
Armstrong Close **20** F3
Arran Way **7** A2
Arrow Drive **29** C2
Arrow Road......................**3** D3
Arthur Way **20** H2
Arundel Close **16** G4
Ash Grove*, Gower St. **12** H2
Ash Lea Drive **6** H5
Ash Road (Bridgnorth) **25** B2
Ash Road (Donnington) **6** H3

Ashbourne Close **16** E3
Ashbourne Drive **28** E2
Ashcroft............................**25** B3
Ashdale Road **12** F1
Ashdown Court **10** E1
Ashdown Lane **1** D5
Ashfields (Albrighton) **29** C2
Ashfields (Oakengates)......**12** F3
Ashford Close **11** C1
Ashgrove **29** C3
Ashlea Court....................**28** G2
Ashley Court*, Chapel St...**15** D4
Ashley Road **12** H3
Ashley View **28** E2
Ashmore Close **7** B2
Ashmore Crescent **23** B3
Ashmore Drive **6** E5
Ashwood Close................**27** C3
Ashworth Way..................**24** F5
Aspen Way (Newport)......**24** F5
Aspen Way (Telford)..........**4** E4
Aston Close........................**4** F6
Aston Court Mews **18** H2
Aston Dale **18** H3
Aston Drive **24** E5
Aston Road **18** H3
Aston Street **18** H3
Athersmith Road **16** E3
Athol Drive **12** G3
Atlas Grove **9** D2
Attingham Close **16** H6
Attwood Terrace **15** D3
Audley Avenue **24** G4
Audley Court....................**24** G4
Audley House Mews..........**24** G4

Audley Road 24 F3/G4
Auster Close 4 H5
Avenue Road (Broseley) ..23 C6
Avenue Road (Newport) 24 F4
Avenue Road South 24 G4
Avenue, The 9 A1
Averbury House*,
    Poachers Gate 15 D2
Avon Close 15 D6
Avondale (Dawley Bank) ..15 C1
Avondale (Newport) 24 F2
Avondale Road (Bridgnorth)
    ....25 C3
Avondale Road (Wellington) 9 D3
Aylwin Court 16 E6
Ayr Close 4 H6

B

Baddleys Court 24 F4
Baden Terrace 9 D1
Bader Close 4 H5
Badger Close 16 F5
Badhan Court*, Stadium Way
    ....11 B1
Bagley Drive 3 D6
Bailey Croft 15 C6
Baldwin Webb Avenue 6 H4
Balfour Road 18 H2
Balls Hill 15 C3
Balls Lane 23 B3
Balmoral Drive 28 G1
Bandon Lane 26 E3
Bank Road (Dawley Bank) 15 D2
Bank Road (Wellington) 10 G2
Bank Steps 25 D3
Bank Street.........................25 D3
Bank Way 12 E4
Baptist Avenue 15 D1
Barber Street 23 B4
Barberry Close 11 D5
Barclay Close 29 D2
Barclay Court 6 G4
Barkers Court 21 C4
Barkers Lane 29 C5
Barleywood Close 7 A5
Barlow Close 16 G4
Barn Close 7 A5
Barn Road 18 H2
Barnes Wallis Drive 4 H4
Barnet Close 4 E6
Barnett Leasowes ..20 G6/23 C2
Barnfield Court 9 D4
Barnfield Crescent 9 D4
Barnfields 29 B6
Barnmeadow Close 24 G4
Barnmeadow Road............24 G4
Barns, The 24 E6
Barrack Lane 8 H3
Barratt Terrace 11 C5
Barratts Hill 23 A4
Barrington Close 29 C2
Barrington Court 18 H2
Barrow Road.......................23 B6

Barrowstyles Lane 28 F2
Bartholomew Road 15 B1
Bartlett Road.......................15 D5
Bartons Corner*, Bartons Road
    ....27 D4
Bartons Court*, Bartons Road
    ....27 D4
Bartons Lane 27 D4
Bartons Road 27 D4
Batch Lane (Bridgnorth) 26 F1
Batches Lane (Broseley) ..23 C6
Bath Road 20 E5/23 A1
Bayley Road 10 G4
Baylham Close 15 B5
Bayswater Close.................13 B3
Beacon Flats*, Kings Haye Road
    ....10 E3
Beaconsfield (Bridgnorth) ..25 B2
Beaconsfield (Telford) 16 G6
Beames Close 16 E5
Beanhill Cottages 3 C4
Beatty Close 18 H1
Beaufort Close 4 H4
Beaumaris...........................24 F4
Beaumaris Road 24 E4/F4
Beckbury Drive 16 F6
Bedstone Close 16 H6
Beech Close (Newport)......24 F5
Beech Close (Wellington) 9 D1
Beech Drive (Broseley).....23 C5
Beech Drive (Shifnal) 18 G2
Beech Road (Bridgnorth) ..25 B2
Beech Road (Madeley) 20 F4/G4
Beeches, The 3 B5
Beechfields Way..................24 G1
Beechurst Gardens...........29 B2
Beechwood Close..............16 E5
Beechwood Court*, The Lawns
    ....28 F2
Beechwood Road 16 E5
Beedles Close....................21 A1
Beestons Close..................26 E3
Belgrave Crescent 16 F6
Bell Street............................10 F2
Belle Vue Road........20 F5/23 B1
Bellmans Yard....................24 F4
Bellpit Road 11 D6
Belmont Road.........20 F5/23 B1
Belvedere Gardens............23 C3
Bembridge 16 G6
Ben Jones Avenue 24 G2
Bennett Road 21 C3
Bennetts Bank 10 H3
Benthall Lane 23 A4
Benthall View 20 G5/23 C1
Bentlands, The 23 A4
Bentley Cottages 26 H3
Bentleys Road 27 C4
Berberis Road......................4 H5
Berkeley Close 13 B3
Bernards Hill 26 E4
Berrisford Close 28 G3
Berrisford Road 28 F3/G2

Bert Smith Way 28 E1
Berwyn Close 16 G4
Betnell Grove 21 A4
Betton Road 28 G1/G2
Beulah Drive 27 D2
Bevan Close 11 B1
Bevan Way 27 D1
Beveley Road 11 C3/D3
Bickerstaff Court 10 E3
Bilberry Close 11 D6
Birbeck Drive 20 H5/23 D1
Birch Close 27 B4
Birch Meadow 23 B4
Birch Meadow Road 23 B4
Birch Row 23 B4
Birch Tree Close 21 B4
Birchdale Avenue 12 F1
Birchlands 26 F3
Birchlee Close....................13 A4
Birchmore 16 F6
Birchwood Close.................7 A3
Bishopdale 21 B1
Bishops Lane 27 D2
Bishton Court*,
    Ironmasters Way 12 G6
Bishton Road 29 B3
Blackmere Close...............24 E5
Blacksmith Drive 12 E4
Blackstone Drive...............12 H2
Blackthorn Grove 4 E4
Blakemore 21 C1
Blakenham Court 15 B5
Blakeway Close 23 C6
Blenheim Road 4 H5
Blews Hill 15 D3
Blews Hill Court 15 D3
Blithe Close 23 C3
Bloomsbury Court.............6 H2
Blue House Barns.............24 E2
Blue House Lane 29 C1
Bluebell Coppice 11 C4
Bluegate 18 H3
Blythe Gardens...................6 H6
Board Close 12 G2
Boatwell Meadow 10 G1
Boddington Crescent 16 G3
Body Road 6 H1
Bollingale Avenue 12 E2
Boningale Close 16 G6
Border, The............................1 D4
Boscobel Close....................16 H6
Bostock Close......................3 B5
Bostock Crescent 21 B1
Botany Bay Close 16 E6
Botfield Close (Albrighton) 29 D2
Botfield Close (Telford)....16 G4
Botfield Road 18 H2
Bottom Lane 27 C5
Boughey Road 24 E4
Boulton Grange............16 G4/H4
Bournbrook Gardens.........16 F6
Bournside Drive 21 B1
Bourton Close....................16 G6

Bower Yard.........................20 E5
Bowers Close 25 B2
Bowland Close 11 C5
Bowling Green Lane 29 A2/B2
Bowmanshill Cottages 26 H6
Bowring Grove 10 E3
Boyd Close 2 E3
Bracken Grove 10 G2
Bracken Way.......................24 F2
Brackenfield 21 B1
Bradford Street 18 H3
Bradley Bank*, Sycamore Road
    ....23 A3
Bradley Court 7 A5
Bradley Road 6 H6
Braithwaite Row 10 E3
Bramble Ridge 25 D2
Brambles, The 11 D6
Bramblewood 23 B4
Bramwell Close...................12 G2
Brandlee 15 C4
Brandon Avenue 3 C4
Brandon Grove 4 H4
Brands Farm Way..............16 H3
Brands Meadow 7 A4
Brandywell Road 23 C3
Bratton Cottages 3 C3
Bratton Lane 3 B5
Bratton Road........................3 B4
Bream Close 4 E5
Brecknock Court 10 H1
Bredon Close 29 C2
Brereton 21 C1
Breton Park Mobile Homes..7 B2
Briarwood 16 F6/G6
Brick Kiln Bank 20 G2
Brick Kiln Way.....................7 A4
Brickhill Lane 11 D2
Bricklin Mews 11 C1
Bridge Bank 20 E6/23 A2
Bridge Close 6 E6
Bridge Road (Broseley)
    ....20 E6/23 A4
Bridge Road (Horsehay)....15 A5
Bridge Road (Mkt. Dray.) ..27 C2
Bridge Road (Wellington) ..10 E1
Bridge Square......................6 E6
Bridge Street (Bridgnorth)..25 D3
Bridge Street (Oakengates)12 F3
Bridge Terrace 24 E3
Bridgeway 7 A3
Bridgnorth Bypass
    ....25 A3/B4/26 E5
Bridgnorth Road (Broseley)
    ....23 B5/B6
Bridgnorth Road (Madeley)
    ....21 B1/B2/D3
Bridgnorth Road (Shifnal) ..18 E6
Bridgwater Close 16 E5
Bridgwood 16 G6
Bridle Court 21 A3
Bridle Road 21 A4
Bridle Terrace 21 A4

Bridleway, The 27 D2
Briery Bank.......................20 G3
Briggs Way 12 G1
Brimstree Drive.................18 G4
Brindley Close 29 C2
Brindley Ford 21 B1
Bristol Place*, Eagle La. ...29 B6
Britannia Way 11 B1
Britten Court*, Roseway 10 F2
Broad Meadow Lane 20 G3
Broad Oaks......................16 H4
Broadstone Mews............20 H1
Broadway (Ketley) 11 B2
Broadway (Newport).........24 G4
Broadway (Shifnal) 18 G3
Broadway Avenue..............6 E5
Broadway Close 18 G2
Brock Hollow....................15 C4
Brockford Glade 3 C4
Brockton 8 G3
Brockton Way 21 D2
Brockwood Copse 3 C5
Bromley Way 12 G3
Bronte Close 9 D1
Brook Hollow....................25 D1
Brook House 24 F3
Brook Meadow 3 C3
Brook Road.......................21 C3
Brookdale (Hadley)...........11 A1
Brookdale (Shifnal)...........18 G2
Brookes Road...................23 C6
Brookfield (Stirchley) 16 G5
Brookfields (Mkt. Dray.) 27 A3
Brooklands Avenue 18 G4
Brooklands Road 29 D2
Brookside 7 A3
Brookside Avenue (Newport)
...............................24 F5
Brookside Avenue (Telford)
.......................16 F6/21 B1
Brookside Centre 16 G6
Brookside Close 18 G2
Brookvale Road 13 A4
Broom Drive 11 D6
Broomfield Close 24 E3
Broomfield Place...............24 E3
Broomfield Road (Admaston)
...............................3 B5
Broomfield Road (Newport)
...............................24 E3
Broomhurst Way 7 B3
Broseley Road 25 C1
Brunel Road 16 E2
Brunlees Drive 16 G4
Bryony Rise 16 H4
Bryony Way 13 A4
Buchan House*, Poachers Gate
...............................15 D2
Buckingham Crescent........16 F6
Buckland Walk 24 F1
Buildwas Bank 19 C2
Buildwas Lane 19 A2
Buildwas Road (Ironbridge)19 A3

Buildwas Road (Wellington) 3 D6
Bullrush Glade 12 G2
Bungalows, The 6 H3
Buntingsdale Road 27 B4
Burcot Row 9 A2
Burfield Court*,
    Maurice Lee Avenue ..12 E2
Burford 21 C1
Burgage Close 28 F2
Burgage Court..................24 F4
Burgage, The 28 E2
Burleigh Close 16 G6
Burlington Close 16 E5
Burlington*, Newport Rd. ..18 H1
Burnell Road......................3 C5
Burnside 21 B1
Burnt Hall Lane 21 B3
Burroughs Bank 20 F1/F2
Burton Close.....................15 C3
Burton Street 15 C3
Burtondale 21 C1
Bush Avenue 16 E4
Bush Close (Albrighton) 29 C2
Bush Close (Telford)...........4 C5
Bush Hill 15 A5
Bushfield Road 29 C2
Butler Court 12 H2
Buttercross 28 E2
Buttercup Close 16 G5
Buttermere Drive...............12 H4
Buttery Grove 12 F2
Buttonwood Glade 11 C4
Butts Road (Mkt. Dray.) 27 D3
Butts Road (Telford) 3 D3
Buxton Road 16 E3
Byron Close 27 C4

C

Cactus Drive 4 H5
Cadfael Drive 16 E6
Cadman Drive 13 B5
Caernarvon Close 28 F1
Calcott 16 H5
Calcutts Road...................23 C3
Calcutts, The*, Calcutts Road
...............................23 C3
Calder Close 7 B4
Caldera Road 11 C1
Caldercrofts 24 G3
Calluna Road 13 B4
Calverhall 16 H5
Cambrian Row 10 F1
Camellia Drive..................13 B4
Campbell Close 25 B3
Campbell Road 28 F1
Campion Drive 7 A4
Canal Side 6 G6
Candleberry Meadow 11 C4
Cankhorn, The 25 D5
Cann Hall Drive 26 E3
Cann Hall Road 26 E3
Canonbie Lea 20 H4
Canongate 12 F3

Canterbury Close 7 B4
Cantreyn Drive 25 B2
Cape Fold*, Cape Street....23 A4
Cape Street......................23 A4
Capewell Road 5 D6
Cappoquin Drive...............12 G2
Captain Webb Drive 15 C3
Captains Meadow 11 D6
Captains Road 25 C4
Caradoc Flats*, Kings Haye Rd.
...............................10 E3
Careswell Gardens............18 G4
Carlisle Close 5 A5
Carlton Drive 13 A3
Carmarthen Green 10 H1
Carnoustie Drive 21 B6
Carpenters Row 20 E3
Cart Gate 10 E2
Cartway............................25 D3
Carvers Close 10 E3
Carvers Road 23 B5
Carwood 16 H5
Cashworth Cottages 29 D2
Castle Acre Road 5 A5
Castle Farm Way 13 B3
Castle Hill 29 C5
Castle Hill Walk (1) 25 D3
Castle Houses 5 C6
Castle Lane 5 C6
Castle Mews*, Stafford St. 12 H3
Castle Road 15 D6
Castle Street 5 C6/11 B1
Castle Terrace 25 D3
Castle View 11 D3
Castlecroft 16 H5
Castlecroft Gardens 26 F4
Castlefields 16 H5
Castlefields Way 16 E6/21 A1/A2
Catherton 16 H5
Catherton Close 29 A5
Catherton Park*, Catherton Rd.
...............................29 B5
Catherton Road 29 A4
Catstree 16 H6
Catterick Close 4 H6
Caughley Close 23 C6
Caughley Road 23 C6
Cavan Drive 15 D1
Cavell Close 4 G5
Cavendish Close 12 F3
Cayton 16 H6
Cecil Close 15 D2
Cedar Close (Mkt. Dray.) ..27 D3
Cedar Close (Overdale) 11 C5
Cedar Drive......................29 C2
Cedarwood Drive 7 A3
Celandine Way 7 A4
Cemetery Road 15 D1
Cemetery Road 27 D2
Central Avenue 11 A2
Central Court 25 D3
Central Square 1 D5
Chainmakers Gate 21 B1

Chalice Close 7 B3
Chancel Drive 27 C2/C3
Chantry Close 23 B3
Chapel Bank 6 G6
Chapel End 5 C2
Chapel Grove 6 G6
Chapel Lane (Aqueduct) 21 A1
Chapel Lane (Bridgnorth) ..26 H6
Chapel Lane (Broseley) 23 A4
Chapel Road (Jackfld.)
...................20 H6/23 D2
Chapel Road (Ironbridge)
...................20 F5/23 B1
Chapel Street (Dawley)......15 D4
Chapel Street (Oakengates)
...............................12 F3
Chapel Street (St. Georges)
...............................12 H3
Chapel Terrace...................6 G6
Chapmans Close 16 F6
Charborough Court 12 E3
Charlecote Park 11 C5
Charles Avenue 29 B2/B3
Charles Road 10 H3
Charles Street 6 G6
Charlesway......................27 D4
Charlton Row*, Charlton Street
...............................10 E1
Charlton Street (Oakengates)
...............................12 E3
Charlton Street (Wellington)
...............................10 E1
Charter Court 28 F2
Chartwell Road 10 H3
Chatford 16 H5
Cheapside 18 G3
Checkley Lane 13 A2
Chelmarsh 16 H6
Cheltenham Court 4 H6
Cheney Hill Court*, Severn Dr.
...............................3 D6
Chepstow Drive 4 H6
Cherrington 16 G5
Cherry Grove 11 D5
Cherry Orchard.................15 D2
Cherry Tree Hill.................20 E2
Cherry Way 28 F1
Cherrybrook Drive.............23 B3
Cheshire Close 20 H5/23 D1
Cheshire Coppice Cottages 3 B4
Cheshire Coppice Lane 5 A4
Cheshire Gardens............28 E2
Cheshire Street.................28 E2
Chesnut Road...................27 C4
Chesterfield Road 16 E3
Chesterton 16 H5
Chestnut Drive (Trench) 6 E5
Chestnut Drive (Wellington) 9 D1
Chestnut Terrace 5 C6
Cheswell Drive 8 F3
Chetwynd Close 16 G6
Chetwynd End...................24 F3
Chetwynd Grove 24 F3

Chetwynd Road **24** E1
Chichester Drive **4** H4
Chilcombe Drive **13** B4
Chilcott Drive **21** D3
Child Pit Lane **8** H1
Childe Road **29** B5
Chiltern Gardens **15** C3
Chirbury **16** H5
Chiswick Court **6** H2
Chockleys Drive **11** A1
Chockleys Meadow............**11** A1
Christ Church Lane...........**27** C4
Christine Avenue **10** E3
Church Alley **23** C5
Church Close **21** B4
Church Hill **20** E5/**23** A1
Church Hill Lane **15** A1
Church Lane (Lit. Wen.)....**19** A2
Church Lane (Bridgnorth) ..**25** A2
Church Lane (Sheriff.) **14** G2
Church Meadow (Lilleshall) **8** G5
Church Meadow (Shifnal)..**18** G3
Church Parade **12** F2
Church Road (Albrighton) ..**29** B3
Church Road (Centre) **1** A5/A6
Church Road (Coalbrkdale.)
........................**20** E3/**22** F5
Church Road (Dawley)
........................**15** D2/**16** E2
Church Road (Donnington)..**7** A4
Church Road (Jackfld.)
........................**20** H6/**23** D2
Church Road (Lilleshall)
.........................**7** C1/**8** F6
Church Road (Snedshill) ..**12** G5
Coalport Close **23** D5
Church Road (Trench) **6** F5
Church Street (Bridgnorth) **25** D3
Church Street (Broseley) ..**23** B5
Church Street (Cleo. Mort.)
.............................**29** C6
Church Street (Hadley) **11** B1
Church Street (Madeley)...**21** B4
Church Street (Mkt. Dray.) **28** E3
Church Street (Oakengates)
..............................**12** F3
Church Street (Shifnal)......**18** G4
Church Street (St. Georges)
........................**12** H3/**13** A3
Church Street (Wellington) **10** F2
Church Walk (Dawley) **15** D5
Church Walk (Donnington) ..**6** H4
Church Walk (Wellington) ..**10** F2
Churchill Court **15** D3
Churchill Drive...................**12** F4
Churchill Road **10** G3
Churchward Close **13** A4
Churchward Drive.............**11** C6
Churchway **16** H5
Churncote **16** H5
Cittings Jitty*, Quarry Rd... **23** A3
Clanbrook **16** H5
Claremont Drive **25** C2
Claremont Mews **10** F1

Clares Lane Close **11** D5
Claverley Drive **16** G6
Clee Hill Court*, Severn Drive
.....................................**3** D6
Clee Rise **19** A2
Clee View Road **25** B2
Clematis Drive **4** H5
Cleveland Close **15** B4
Cliff Gardens*, Cliff Road ..**25** D3
Cliff Road **25** D3
Clifford Road.....................**27** D4
Clift Crescent **9** D2
Clive Gardens **28** E3
Clive Road **28** E3
Clockmills **29** B2
Cloisters, The **12** E2
Close, The (Coalbrkdale.)..**19** D2
Close, The (Newport) **24** F6
Close, The*, Smithy Bank ..**23** B5
Clover Grove.....................**16** H4
Clowes Drive.....................**16** H3
Clun Close **3** D6
Clunbury Road **3** D6
Clydesdale Drive...............**15** B4
Coach Central.....................**1** C5
Coach Road **20** E3
Coachman Meadow **3** D4
Coachwell Close **1** A6
Coalbrookdale Road
   (Coalbrkdale.) **19** C1
Coalbrookdale Road (Lit. Wen.)
...................................**19** B2
Coalford **20** G6/**23** C2
Coalmoor Road.................**15** A4
Coalport Close **23** D5
Coalport High Street..........**22** G5
Coalport Road (Broseley) ..**23** C5
Coalport Road (Coalport)
............................**22** F5/H6
Coalport Road (Madeley)
.............................**21** A6/B5
Cobwell Road **23** A3
Cockshutt Lane **23** B4
Cockshutt Road (Oakengates)
..............................**12** F3
Cockshutt Road (Wrkwdine. Wd.)
.............................**12** G1
Colemere Drive.................**10** E1
Coleridge Close **27** C5
College Close **29** B5
College Court **26** F4
College Lane **10** G1
Collett Way **13** A4
Colliers Way (Centre) **1** A3/B2
Colliers Way (The Rock)....**11** D6
Colliford Close...................**13** B3
Collingwood Court **18** H1
Collins Close.....................**23** C5
Colridge Court.....................**7** A4
Columbine Way **7** A4
Combermere Court **28** F2
Combermere Drive **10** E1
Commercial Way................**12** F3

Common, The (Donnington) **6** H5
Common, The (Horsehay) **15** B3
Concorde **15** C2
Conduit Lane **25** B4
Coney Green Way **4** E4
Coneybury View **23** C5
Coniston Drive **2** H1
Connomara Meadow **15** B4
Conroy Drive.....................**15** C3
Constable Drive **3** C4
Constitution Hill **10** F1
Cooke Drive **16** E5
Cooper Close **13** B5
Copper Beech Road **11** A2/B2
Copperfield Drive **6** H3
Copperfield Road **25** B2
Coppice Close **21** C4
Coppice Drive (Newport)...**24** F1
Coppice Drive (Wrkwdine. Wd.)
..................................**12** G1
Coppice Green **18** H3
Coppice Road **18** H1
Coppice, The (Centre) **1** A2
Coppice, The (Mkt. Dray.)..**27** D2
Corbet Court **28** E3
Corbet Grove **27** B6
Corbett Close **15** D6
Cordingley Way **6** G5
Cordy Lane **29** D1
Corfield Crescent **12** E2
Cornbrook.........................**16** H5
Corndean Meadow **11** C6
Cornflower Grove **11** C4
Cornmell Lea **24** G3
Cornwallis Drive **18** H2
Coronation Crescent.........**21** B3
Coronation Drive **7** A3/A4
Coronation Place **11** C3
Coronation Terrace **12** G2
Corve Walk **12** H1
Cote Road **3** D3
Cotswold Drive (Albrighton)
....................................**29** D2
Cotswold Drive (Telford)....**16** G3
Cottage Close **21** C4
Cottage Drive **18** G4
Cottage Farm Close **21** B4
Coughs Jitty*, Quarry Rd. **23** A3
Council Houses.................**22** E6
Cound Close **4** E6
Country Meadows.............**27** B3
Court Road **21** B2
Court Street **21** B3
Court, The (Sutton Hill) **21** B6
Courtland Drive **6** E6
Courts, The (Albrighton) ...**29** C3
Cow Wood **11** C4
Crackshall Lane **20** E1
Craft Way **7** A2
Craig Walk **25** D4
Cranage Crescent **9** D2
Cranmere **16** H5
Crawstone Close **12** H2

Crescent Road (Hadley)
.............................**11** A2/B1
Crescent Road (Wellington)
....................................**10** E1
Crescent, The (Donnington) **6** H4
Crescent, The (Lawley)......**15** A2
Crescent, The (Newport)....**24** F6
Crescent, The (Sheriff.) **14** H1
Crest Road **13** A3
Crest, The **1** A2
Cricket Fields*, Cherrybrook Dr.
.... **23** B3
Cricket Meadow **25** C3
Cricketers Lane **13** A3
Croft Fold **15** D2
Croft Way **27** D2
Croft, The (Bridgnorth) **26** E3
Crofters View **19** A1
Crofts, The (Madeley)........**20** G3
Cromwell House*,
   Poachers Gate **15** D2
Cross Bank (Stirchley) **17** A5
Cross Bank*, High Street ..**24** F3
Cross Road........................**29** B3
Cross Street **28** F3
Crosskeys Lane **11** A1
Crowdale Road **3** C4
Crown Street (Dawley) **15** D4
Crown Street (Wellington)..**10** F2
Crowther Flats*, Glebe St. **10** F2
Cuckoo Oak Green **21** C3
Cuckoos Rest **21** B1
Culmington **16** H5
Cumberland Close **23** B4
Cumberland Mews **10** H1
Curdale Close **29** A6
Curie Croft **4** G5
Curlew Drive **4** H6
Curriers Lane **18** H2
Cygnet Drive **21** C1
Cypress Close **27** D3
Cyril Hayward Court **11** B1

D

Daddlebrook **16** H2
Dairy Close **28** F2
Daisy Bank Drive **12** H1
Dalby Close **4** G6
Dale Acre Way..............**2** E4/F6
Dale End **19** D5/**23** A1
Dale End Court*, Dale End **19** D5
Dale Road..........................**20** E4
Dale View*, Wellington Rd.**20** E3
Dale, The **24** F6
Dalebrook Drive **7** A5
Dalefield Drive.....................**3** B5
Dalelands **2** F5
Dalelands Estate **27** D3/D4
Dalelands West **27** D4
Dalford Court **2** E5
Dallamoor **2** G6
Damson Drive **11** D5
Danesbridge **25** D5

Danesford 2 F6
Daniels Cross 24 G2
Darby Road 19 D2/20 E3
Dark Lane (Broseley) 23 B5
Dark Lane (Newport)..........24 E6
Dark Lane (Telford)............16 F3
Dark Lane Drive 16 F2
Darliston 16 H2
Darwin Close.....................28 E1
Darwin Road 4 F6
Dashwood Drive 4 E4
Dashwood House*,
    Poachers Gate 15 D2
Davenham Walk 15 C1
Davenport Drive 3 C4
Dawley Bank.....................15 D2
Dawley Green Way 15 C3/D2
Dawley Road (Arleston)
..........................10 G3/15 A1
Dawley Way 16 F4
Dawson Fayre 27 D1
Daywell...............................2 G5
Dean Close (Mkt. Dray.) 27 C2
Dean Close (Priorslee) 13 A3
Dean Square 1 D4
Dean Street 1 D5
Decker Hill 14 H5
Decmar Road*, Estate Rd. 26 H4
Dee Close 4 E5
Deepdale 2 F6
Deepfield 15 D5
Deepfield Road.................15 D5
Deer Park Drive................24 F1
Deer Park Road 4 E6
Deer Park Way 13 A1
Deercote 2 E6
Deightons Close 25 C4
Delamere Close 11 C5
Delaware Avenue 29 B3
Delbury Court 2 E6
Delph, The 16 G4
Delphside 23 B5
Delphside Court*, Delphside
..........................23 B5
Derwent Drive 13 A4/A5
Detton Court*, Maurice Lee Av.
..........................12 E2
Deuxhill Close...................15 D2
Dickins Road 6 G6
Dinchope Drive 2 F5
Dingle View.......................25 C1
Dinthill..............................16 H2
Doctors Lane 25 D3
Doddington 2 G6
Doddlecote Close 16 G5
Dodmoor Grange 16 G3
Dog Kennel Lane 28 F3
Domas Way 15 D2
Donington Lane 29 C1
Donnerville Close 3 D6
Donnerville Drive 3 D6
Donnerville Gardens 3 C6
Donnington Drive 6 G1

Donnington Way.................6 G1
Donnington Wood Way ..7 A3/A6
Dorchester Drive.................7 B4
Dorran Place 12 G4
Doseley Road 15 C5
Doseley Road North 15 C4
Dothill Court*, Severn Dr. 3 D6
Double Gates Flats*,
    Alexandra Road 27 D3
Dove Close 11 C1
Dove Court.............20 G5/23 B1
Dovedale Fold...................16 E3
Dovehouse Court 23 C5
Dover Drive 5 A5
Downfields 24 G1
Downmead 2 F5
Downton Court 2 E6
Draper Court 10 F1
Draycott 16 H2
Drayton Grove 28 E2
Drayton Mill Court 28 E2
Drayton Road 18 H1
Drayton Way 15 D3
Drovers Way......................24 H2
Drummery Lane 9 A1
Drummond Close 20 F3
Duchess Drive 25 B2
Duckett Drive 15 C5
Dudmaston 2 G6
Duffryn 2 F4
Duke Street (Broseley) 23 A4
Duke Street (Wellington)....10 F2
Dukes Hill.....................12 E4/F4
Dukes Place 12 H3
Dukes Street (St. Georges)
..........................12 H3
Dukes Way 12 H3
Dulwich Grange 3 B4
Dungarven Drive 24 E4
Dunlin Close 4 H6
Dunmaster Way 16 F6
Dunsheath 2 E4/E5/F4
Dunstone 2 G6
Dunval Close 25 B1
Dunval Road 25 B1/C2
Durrant Road 12 H4
Duxmore Way 15 D2
Dyas Close 18 G4
Dyas Mews.......................18 G4

E

Eagle Court 10 F1
Eagle Lane 29 B6
Earls Drive 21 A1
Earlswood Drive 21 A5
East Avenue 6 G4
East Castle Street..............25 D3
East Road 12 F4
East View (The Humbers)....6 F1
East View (Wrkwdine.) 9 A1
Easthope Coppice 23 B2
Easthope Road 23 B3
Eastwood Drive...................7 A6

Eaton Crescent...........12 G3/G4
Ebenezer Row 25 D4
Ebenezer Steps (2)...........25 D4
Edgmond Park*, Edgmond Rd.
..........................24 E2
Edgmond Road 24 E2
Edinburgh Road 23 B4
Edith Close 16 E6
Edney House*, Poachers Gate
..........................15 D2
Edward Parry Court 15 D1
Edward Terrace 6 E5
Eglantine Close...................7 A4
Eider Drive 4 G4
Elderberry Close 11 D5
Eleanors Close 21 A1
Elim Court 11 A1
Elim Terrace 5 D6
Eliot Close.........................17 A5
Elizabeth Avenue 25 B2
Elizabeth Court 28 E3
Elizabeth Crescent 23 A3
Elizabeth Mews 29 C5
Elkington Close.................24 E4
Ellen Court 10 G2
Ellender Rise 15 C1
Ellesmere Court 24 F4
Ellesmere Grove...............27 C3
Ellis Peters Drive..............16 E6
Ellwand Court 16 E5
Elm Close 24 F5
Elm Drive 27 C3
Elm Road 29 A2
Elm Way..............................6 E6
Elmhurst 26 F3
Elmhurst Coppice 7 A3
Elmpark Drive 9 D1
Elmscourt 3 C5
Elmsdale Crescent 3 B5
Eltham Drive 13 C4
Elvin Close 15 C5
Ely Close 13 C4
Emral Rise 4 E5
Ennerdale Close 12 H4
Entry Bank 7 A2
Epsom Court 4 H6
Ercall Close.........................6 E6
Ercall Gardens 10 E2
Ercall Lane 10 E4
Ercall View 11 C5
Espley Close.....................10 F2
Essex Chase.....................13 A4
Estate Road 26 H4
Euston Way..........................2 F3
Everglade Road 13 A5
Evergreens, The 14 H2
Eversley Cottages 25 C5
Ewart Road..........................6 H5
Exchange Buildings 12 F1
Exeter Drive 10 G1
Eyton Place.......................16 E3
Eyton Road 16 E3
Eyton View 4 E5

F

Fair Lawn 29 C2/C3
Fair Oak 24 F2
Fairburn Road 16 G4
Fairfield 25 B2
Fairfield Court 10 F1
Fairfields Road 28 F1
Fairlawn Court 29 C3
Fairview.............................12 F4
Fairways Drive 20 H5/23 D1
Falcon Flats*, Kings Haye Road
..........................10 E3
Fallow Deer Lawn 24 F1
Fallow Road 3 D4
Far Croft*, North Road 10 E1
Far Vallens 11 C2
Faraday Drive 26 F4
Farcroft Drive 27 C3
Farm Close (Madeley) 21 C4
Farm Close (Mkt. Dray.) ...27 D2
Farm Grove.......................24 E4
Farm Lane (Donnington).....6 H4
Farm Lane (Horsehay) 15 A4
Farm Lodge Grove 16 E2
Farm Meadow Close..........15 A4
Farmlands Road 25 B3
Farmstead Court................9 D3
Farriers Green (Lawley Bank)
..........................15 B1
Farriers Green (Newport) ..24 H3
Fellows Close 15 D6
Fells Orchard 25 D5
Fence Road 15 B3
Fenns Crescent 12 H2
Ferndale Drive 13 A5
Ferney Bank*, Quarry Road
..........................23 A3
Fernwood Close 4 E5
Ferriday Close 20 G3
Ferry Road 22 G5
Festival Gardens 10 G4
Field Close 16 E2
Field Lane 22 H2
Field Road 6 F5
Fieldfare Way 21 A1
Fieldhouse Drive 6 H3/7 A3
Fielding Close...................23 D5
Fields, The 7 A4
Fifth Avenue 12 F5
Finchale Avenue 13 C4
Finger Road 15 D4
Finger, The 16 E5
Finsbury Drive 13 B3
Fireclay Drive 12 H2
Firecrest Drive 4 G6
First Avenue 12 F5
Firtrees 26 F4
Fishers Lock 24 F3
Five Way Flats 28 E4
Flag Leasow.........20 H5/23 D1
Fleming Court 4 G5
Floyer Lane.......................23 A4

Folly, The 24 F6
Forbes Close.....................20 F4
Ford Road 24 E4/E5
Fordhall Cottages 27 A5
Forest Close 3 D3
Forest Road 27 C3
Forester Grove 10 G3
Forester Road...................23 C5
Foresters Close 15 A5
Forge Gate 1 C2
Forsythia Close.................13 B4
Forton Glade......................24 F2
Forton Road 24 F2
Foster Road 25 B1
Fosters Foel 21 B1
Foundry Close*, Reynolds Drive
....12 F3
Foundry Court...................23 B5
Foundry Lane 23 B5
Fountain Drive 12 G3
Four Winds Mobile Homes Park
....23 B4
Fourth Avenue 12 F5
Fowler Close........................4 E6
Fox Avenue 12 H4
Fox Lane............................23 B4
Foxes, The 21 B5
Foxglove Rise....................16 H4
Foxs Covert 3 D4
Frame Lane 15 B5
Freeston Avenue 12 G4
Freeston Terrace 12 H5
Friars Street 25 D3
Frizes Leasowe.................12 E5
Frog Lane*, Frogmore Rd. 28 E2
Frogmore Close.................28 E2
Frogmore Lane*, Frogmore Rd.
....28 E2
Frogmore Place.................28 E2
Frogmore Road.................28 E2
Frome Way........................12 H1
Fryers Close......................29 B5
Fuchsia Close....................13 B4
Fulbeck House*, Poachers Gate
....15 D2
Furlongs Close 29 C4
Furlongs Road 29 C5
Furnace Lane......................6 G4
Furnace Road....................12 G4
Fylingdales Drive 15 C5

Gainsborough Way............3 D4
Garbett Road 21 A1
Garden Close 12 F1
Garfield Road 11 D4
Gatcombe Way..................13 B3
Gate Street.......................12 G3
Gatehouse Close 4 F4
George Chetwood Court....16 E3
George Place 9 D1
George Street (Dawley) 15 C4
George Street*, West St. ..12 G3

Gibbons Close 6 G6
Gibbons Road 6 G5
Gilbert Close 24 E5
Giles Close 3 C4
Gilpin Road 3 B6
Gilwell Grove......................13 B4
Gittens Drive 21 A1
Glade Way 3 D3/D4
Gladstone Court 11 B1
Gladstone House Flats*, High St.
....11 B1
Gladstone Street...............11 B1
Glebe Croft 23 B5
Glebe Flats*, Glebe St. 10 F2
Glebe Street 10 F2
Glebe, The 29 C2
Glebelands, The 6 H5
Glen Brook Road 13 A4
Glen Caravan Park 29 B4
Glen Cottages 11 C2
Glendale 11 A6
Glendale Gardens.............15 A1
Glendale Mews 15 A1
Glendinning Way 20 H4
Glendon Close 27 C3
Gleneagles Close 21 C6
Gloucester Avenue 15 D3
Gloucester Court................4 H4
Glovers Way 3 C3
Goldcrest Grove 4 G4
Goldney Court....................15 B4
Goldstone Drive 25 C2
Golf Links Cottages 10 G2
Golf Links Lane 10 F4
Gooch Close 20 F3
Goodrich Close 7 A3
Goodwood Avenue 26 E4
Goodyear Way 7 A5
Goosefields Close.............28 E3
Gordon House*, Cordingley Way
....6 G5
Gordon Road 6 F5
Goshawk Drive 4 G4
Gosling Park 4 E4
Gough Close 13 B5
Goulbourne Road 12 H3
Gower Close 7 B2
Gower Street 12 H2
Grainger Drive......4 F6/H6/10 H1
Grampian Close 7 A2
Granary Steps 25 D3
Grange Avenue 16 G5
Grange Central 1 D5
Grange Close 16 H6
Grange Cottages 7 D3
Grange Farm Rise 15 D1
Grange Farm View 16 G4
Grange Lane 7 B6/13 B3
Grange Park 29 B2
Grange Road (Albrighton)..29 B2
Grange Road (Ketley Bank)
....12 E5
Granville Avenue...............24 F4

Granville Close 24 F4
Granville Drive 7 B3
Granville Road (Donnington Wd.)
.............................7 A6/C6/13 C1
Granville Road (Newport) ..24 F5
Granville Street.................12 H3
Granville Terrace 11 C1
Granville Villas*, Granville Road
....24 F5
Grasmere Close 12 H4
Gravel Leasowes 20 G1
Gravelly Drive 24 E4
Great Croft 11 D6
Great Hales Street 28 F3
Great Hay Drive 21 B6/22 G5
Great Western Drive 15 B4
Grebe Close 21 D1
Green Acres 12 E4
Green Lane (Albrighton) 29 A3
Green Lane (Newport) 24 E3
Green Man Close 10 G2
Green Way 15 D2
Green, The 8 G5
Greenacres Way 24 E3
Greenaway Place 6 G5
Greenfields 18 H3
Greenfields Court 25 C2
Greenfields Crescent
(Bridgnorth) 25 C2
Greenfields Crescent (Shifnal)
....18 H3
Greenfields Drive 25 C2
Greenfields Lane 27 D2
Greenfields Road 25 C2
Greenfinch Close 4 G6
Greengage Way 7 A3
Greenlea Road 6 F6
Greenvale 24 E6
Greenwood Drive 3 C3
Gregson Walk 15 C2
Grenville Court 18 H2
Gresham Drive 11 B6
Gresley Close 20 F3
Greyfriars 25 D2
Greyhound Hill 12 F4
Grindle Road 22 H4
Grinshill Flats 4 E6
Grizedale Drive 15 C5
Grooms Alley 10 E2
Grooms Lane 22 H3
Grosvenor Court (Mkt. Dray.)
....28 F2
Grosvenor Court (Wellington)
....10 G2
Grosvenor Gardens 18 H3
Grosvenor Road 28 F2
Grotto Road 27 D3
Grove Court*, Grove St. ...12 H3
Grove Crescent.................26 E4
Grove Estate, The 12 H3
Grove Gardens 28 F2
Grove Meadow 29 C5
Grove Road 11 C5

Grove Street 12 H3
Grove Terrace...................26 E3
Grove, The (Hadley) 5 A6
Grove, The (Shifnal) 18 H3
Grovefields 5 A6
Guest Road 23 C6
Guests Close 7 A5
Guinea Close 12 G4
Guisbourne Avenue 3 D3

H

Haddon Place 15 D2
Hadley Gardens 5 A5
Hadley Lodge Road 11 C1
Hadley Park Road 5 A4/A6
Hadley Road (Ketley) 11 C1
Hadley Road (Oakengates)12 E2
Hadley Vallens 11 C1
Hadrian Flats 10 E3
Hafren Road 15 D6
Halcyon Court 7 B3
Hales Court........................14 H1
Halesfield 1..............17 A6/22 E2
Halesfield 2........................22 E2
Halesfield 5........................22 F2
Halesfield 6........................22 E2
Halesfield 7........................22 F3
Halesfield 8........................22 E4
Halesfield 9 ....22 E4/F4
Halesfield 10......................22 E5
Halesfield 11......................22 E5
Halesfield 13......................22 E4
Halesfield 14......................21 D4
Halesfield 15......................22 E4
Halesfield 16......................22 E3
Halesfield 17......................21 D3
Halesfield 18......................21 D3
Halesfield 19......................21 D2
Halesfield 20 ....22 E3
Halesfield 21......................22 E2
Halesfield 22......................22 E1
Halesfield 23......................22 E1
Halesfield 24......................22 E1
Halesfield 25......................17 A6
Halesfield Road 21 C3
Halifax Drive..............4 H6/5 A6
Hall Barn Close 21 A4
Hall Dene 11 A1
Hall Gardens 10 H2
Hall Lane 22 G3
Hall Park Way......................1 B4
Hallcroft Close...................24 E4
Hallcroft Gardens 24 E3
Hamilton Road 15 D5
Hamlet Close 12 E2
Hampton Close..................24 G3
Hampton Court 10 E3
Hampton Drive (Mkt. Dray.)27 D1
Hampton Drive (Newport)..24 G3
Hampton Hill..............9 D4/10 E3
Hancocks Drive 12 F3
Hanover Court 21 B3
Harcourt Drive 24 G3

Harding Close......................6 G4
Harebell Glade 16 H4
Harley Close 3 D5
Harley Way 25 B3
Harp Lane..........................15 D5
Harrington Heath 3 D3
Harris Green 23 A4
Harris Lane 20 G5/23 C1
Harris Terrace...................11 C5
Harrison Close 20 H5/23 D1
Harrison Gardens*, Dawley Rd.
....10 G3
Hartley Close 11 D5
Hartmann Close 29 B6
Hartsbridge 12 E3
Hartshill.............................12 E3
Hartshill Avenue 12 E3
Hartshorne Court 15 D3
Hartwood Close 24 F1
Harvey Crescent...............10 H3
Harvington Close 4 F6
Haughmond Court 4 E5
Haughton Close 25 B2
Haughton Drive 18 G3
Haughton Lane 18 G2
Haughton Road 17 D1/18 F1
Havenwood.......................17 A5
Havisham Court 24 E3
Hawkshaw Close..............12 F3
Hawkstone Avenue 24 F4
Hawksworth Road 12 G5
Hawshaw Close 16 G4
Hawthorn Place 6 H3
Hawthorn Road...................6 H4
Hawthorn Way...................28 F1
Hawthorne Close 12 E4
Hawthorns, The 25 C4
Hay, The 11 C6
Haybridge Avenue........11 A1/A2
Haybridge Hall Bungalows*,
    Haybridge Rd...10 H3/11 A1
Haybridge Hall Flats*,
    Haybridge Rd...10 H3/11 A1
Haybridge Road 10 H3/11 A1
Haybrook Terrace 23 A4
Haycocks Close 4 E5
Hayes Road 10 G4
Hayes, The 27 C4
Haygate Court*, Haygate Road
....10 E2
Haygate Drive East..............9 D3
Haygate Drive West 9 D3
Haygate Grove 10 E2
Haygate Road......................9 D3
Hayward Avenue (Donnington)
....6 H4/H5
Hayward Avenue (St. Georges)
....12 H4
Haywards Parade 12 E2
Hazel View 26 F4
Hazel Way 12 G4
Hazelwood Drive...............20 H1
Heath Close*, Ludlow Rd...29 A6

Heath Court*, Maurice Lee Av.
....12 E2
Heath Hill.....................15 B2/C3
Heath Road..........................4 E6
Heather Drive 10 G2
Heatherdale 4 G6
Heathlands Close 12 G3
Heathwood Road 24 E4
Hedingham Road 5 A5
Hem Lane 22 F1
Hendrie Close 11 B3
Hengrave Meadow 11 C6
Henley Drive (Newport) 24 G3
Henley Drive (Trench)..........6 F6
Herbert Avenue 9 D3
Hereford Drive 13 C4
Hermitage Close 26 E3
Hermitage Heights 26 E3
Hermitage Way 20 H5/23 D1
Heron Close 21 D1
Heron Way 24 G2
Hertford Close 4 G6
Hesba Close 9 D2
Heslop 21 D3
Heywood Lonsdale Court ..10 F2
Hiatt Avenue 10 F1
Hickman Road 26 H3
High Meadows 24 G3
High Mount 6 H5
High Street (Albrighton)29 B2/C3
High Street (Bridgnoth)......25 D3
High Street (Broseley).......23 B4
High Street (Cleo. Mort.)...29 B6
High Street (Dawley).........15 D4
High Street (Hadley) 11 B1
High Street (Ironbridge)
.............................20 E5/23 A1
High Street (Lightmoor)......15 A6
High Street (Madeley)........21 B4
High Street (Mkt. Dray.) ...28 F3
High Street (Newport) 24 F3
High Street (Shifnal) 18 H2
High Street (Wellington) 10 F2
High View 15 C2
Highfield (Lawley) 15 A1
Highfield (Newport) 24 F6
Highfields (Mkt. Dray.) 27 D3
Highgate Drive 13 B3
Highgrove Meadows 13 B4
Highland Lea......................15 B4
Highland Road (Newport) ..24 E4
Highlands Road (Bridgnorth)
....25 B4
Highpoint...........................19 B1
Highway View 11 A3
Hilda Hooke Close 21 C4
Hill Fold 15 D1
Hill Road (Donnington) 6 H1
Hill Road (Overdale)..........11 C5
Hill Street 12 G3
Hill Top Road 11 D3
Hillcrest Road 12 G3
Hillfield Rise 27 C4

Hills Cottages, The 28 H3
Hills Lane Drive.................21 C4
Hillside (Donn. Wd.)...........7 A5
Hillside (Ironbridge)..20 F5/23 B1
Hillside (Lilleshall)...............8 G5
Hillside Avenue 26 E5
Hillside Close 10 H4
Hillside East 8 G5
Hillside Road 12 F4
Hilly Bank 25 C4
Hilton Close 16 G6
Hilton Terrace 12 G2
Hinkshay Road 16 E5
Hinsley Mill Lane 28 G2
Hobbins, The 26 G3/H3
Hockley Bank 23 A5
Hockley Road 23 B5
Hodge Bower 20 E5/F5/23 A1/B1
Holbourn Crescent 13 B3
Holland Drive 7 B3
Hollies Road 9 D1
Hollies, The.......................27 C4
Hollinsgate 2 E4
Hollinswood Road.............22 F1
Hollow, The.......................15 D3
Holly Close 27 C3
Holly Court 15 C6
Holly Road 15 C6/D6
Hollybirch Grove 12 G4
Hollybush Road 25 C3
Hollyhurst Road 12 E1
Hollyoak Grove 13 A4
Holme Court 4 F6
Holmer Farm Road 16 H6
Holmer Lane 16 H6
Holt Coppice Road 3 B4
Holyhead Road (Centre)......2 F1
Holyhead Road (Ketley)11 A3/B3
Holyhead Road (Oakengates)
....12 E3/G4
Holyhead Road (Shifnal) ..18 H5
Holyhead Road (Wellington)
.............................9 C3/10 E3
Holywell Lane 20 F1
Hombersley Terrace 11 C3
Homelands, The*, Mossey Green
....11 D4
Hook Cottages 25 B1
Hook Farm Drive...............25 B1
Hook Farm Road 25 B2
Hookacre Grove 13 A4
Hookfield, The...................25 B2
Hopeshay Close 16 G6
Hopkins Heath 3 D3
Hordley Court*, Hordley Rd. 3 D6
Hordley Road 3 D6
Hornbeam Close...............10 H3
Horne Road 6 H1
Hornet Way.......................11 D5
Horsechestnut Drive 3 D3
Horsegrove Hill*, The Mall 26 E4
Horsehay Common 15 B3
Horsehoe Paddock 15 B2

Horton Court 6 E3
Horton Lane.............5 C2/D4/D5
Horton Road 5 D5
Hortonwood 1 ....5 D4/D
Hortonwood 2 ....5 D5
Hortonwood 7 ....5 D5/6 E4
Hortonwood 8 ....6 E4
Hortonwood 10 ....5 D4
Hortonwood 30 ....5 C4/D4
Hortonwood 31 ....5 D4
Hortonwood 32 ....5 D4
Hortonwood 33 ....6 E4
Hortonwood 35 ....5 D4
Hortonwood 37 ....6 E4
Hortonwood 40 ....5 D4
Hortonwood 50 ....6 E3
Hortonwood 60 ....5 C3
Hoskens Close 15 C3
Hospital Lane 27 C3
Hospital Street 26 E4
Houlston Close 12 H2
Houseman Close 16 E6
Howle Close 16 G5
Hudson Close 12 F1
Humber Lane 6 F1
Humber Way 6 F1/G1
Hungry Lane*, Highfields ..27 D3
Hunters Rise 15 B1
Huntingdon Close 15 C2
Huntingdon Drive 15 C2
Huntsman Way 15 D3
Huntsmans Close 25 B3
Hurleybrook Way ...10 H1/11 A1
Hurst Close 23 C6
Hurst, The 29 C5
Hutchinson Way 11 C3
Hyde Close 7 B3

Ice House Close 4 F4
Idsall Court 18 H3
Idsall Crescent 18 H2
Incline, The (Coalport) 22 G5
Incline, The (Ketley) 11 C3
Incline, The (Lilleshall) 8 F1
Ingestre Close...................24 E4
Innage Crescent 25 C2
Innage Croft 18 G3
Innage Gardens 25 C2
Innage Lane 25 C2
Innage Road......................18 G3
Innes Avenue 12 E3
Iris Crescent 12 G1
Ironbridge Bypass.............20 E1
Ironbridge Road (Jackfld.)
.............................20 G6/23 C2
Ironbridge Road (Broseley)
....23 C5
Ironbridge Road (Madeley)
.............................20 G4/H4
Ironmasters Way.................1 D3
Ironstone Close 12 H2
Isiah Avenue.....................15 C1

Islington Close 24 F2
Ivatt Close.........................16 E5
Ivor Thomas Road 12 H4
Ivy Grove 10 E2
Ivy House Paddocks 11 B2

J

Jabe Davies Close 12 H4
Jackfield Mill......................22 G5
Jackson Avenue 23 A4
James Clay Court.............11 A2
James Close (Sheriff.) 14 H1
James Close (Trench).........6 F6
James Nelson Crescent 6 G5
James Way..........................6 G4
Japonica Drive 4 H5
Jarman Drive 15 B5
Jasmin Close 11 D5
Jay Drive 4 G6
Jellicoe Crescent 18 H1
Jenny Trevors Lane 28 H1
Jews Jitty*, Quarry Road ..23 A3
Jiggers Bank......................19 D1
Jockey Bank 20 G5/23 C1
John Broad Avenue 10 G3
John Street........................18 G3
Johnston Road 15 D3
Johnstone Close 6 G6/12 G1
Joseph Rich Avenue..........21 A4
Jubilee Avenue 6 H3
Jubilee Terrace....................5 D6
Juniper Drive 6 E6/12 E1
Juniper Row 24 F5

K

Kearton Terrace 11 C1
Keay Flats*, High Street 10 F2
Keep, The 20 H4
Keepers Crescent.............12 H1
Kemberton Drive...............21 C3
Kemberton Link.................22 F2
Kemberton Road................22 E3
Kendal Court*, Ironmaster Way
....12 G6
Kenilworth Close 28 F2
Kensington Way 12 F3
Kenway Drive 6 H6
Kestrel Close 24 G1
Kestrel Court 4 G6
Kesworth Drive 13 B5
Ketley Brook 11 A3
Ketley Dingle.....................11 A4
Ketley Town 11 B4
Ketley Vallens...................11 C2
Kettlemore Lane 14 H1
Kew Gardens 13 B4
Kidderminster Road 26 E5
Kielder Square 1 D5
Kiln Bank Crescent 28 E4
Kiln Bank Road 28 E4
King Charles Barns 21 B4
King Charles Way.............25 D2
King Street (Broseley) ..23 A3/A4

King Street (Dawley)..........15 D4
King Street (Wellington) 10 F1
Kingfisher Close 24 G1
Kingfisher Way 4 G6
Kings Avenue 27 C3
Kings Court*, Kings St. 10 F1
Kings Haye Road 10 E3
Kings Head Residential Park
....24 E3
Kings Loade 25 D4
Kingsland 10 H3/H4
Kingsley Drive.....................6 H2
Kingston Road 6 F6
Kingsway Crescent...........10 H3
Kingswood Road 29 D3
Knightsbridge Crescent......16 F6
Knowle Bank 18 E2
Knowle Wood View............16 H3
Knowle, The 23 C3
Kynnersley Drive...............10 F5

L

Laburnum Close (Mkt. Dray.)
....28 F1
Laburnum Close (Shifnal)..18 G2
Laburnum Drive 21 B4
Laburnum Road 12 E1
Lacon Close 29 A5
Lacon Court 29 A5
Ladbrook Drive 12 G4
Ladycroft 10 F1
Ladygrove.........................15 C2
Ladywood 20 F6/23 B2
Lake End Drive 21 D1
Lambeth Drive (Priorslee)..13 C3
Lambeth Drive (Stirchley) ..16 F6
Lamp Shutt Flats...............28 F3
Lancaster Avenue.............15 D3
Lancaster Court 15 D3
Lancaster Place 15 D3
Landau Court*, Tan Bank ..10 F2
Landy Close 6 H2
Lanesend 26 H1
Laneside 7 B3
Langer Court......................12 H3
Langholm Green 20 H4
Langland Road 29 B5
Langley Crescent 16 E4
Langley Fields*, Hinksay Road
....16 E4
Langley Fold 16 E4
Lapwing Gate 13 A5
Lapworth Way 24 G3
Larch Wood 16 H4
Lark Rise 12 G2
Larkrise Field 14 H1
Larks Rise.........................29 A6
Larkspur Glade 16 H4
Laurel Drive.......................24 F3
Laurel Lane.......................11 C5
Laurel Villas 25 C5
Laurels, The*, Legges Hill..23 A3

Lavington View 26 E4
Lawford Close...................20 H1
Lawley.................................15 A1
Lawley Drive............11 A5/15 A2
Lawley Furnaces 10 H6
Lawley Gate 15 A2
Lawn Central 1 D4
Lawndale 6 G4
Lawns Wood 16 F2
Lawns, The (Mkt. Dray.) 28 F2
Lawns, The (Wellington) 10 F1
Lawrence Road 9 D2
Lawton Farm Close.............4 H5
Lawton Farm Way................4 H5
Lawton Road 18 H3
Lawtons Lane 20 E2
Lea Court 4 F6
Lea View 29 A5
Leadon Close 20 H1
Leasowe Green 20 G1
Leasowes Close 25 B3
Leaton Drive 4 E6
Lee Court*, Queen Street ..10 E1
Lee Dingle 21 A5
Leegate Avenue 4 H5/H6/5 A6
Leegomery Cottages*,
    Pool Farm Avenue 4 H6
Leegomery Road 10 F1
Lees Farm Drive
.....................20 H5/21 A5/23 D1
Leeses Close 3 C3
Legges Hill 23 A3
Legges Way 21 B5
Leicester Way......................4 H6
Leigh Road 24 E4
Lennock Road......................6 F5
Leonard Close 6 G5
Leonard Street 12 F2
Leveson Close 12 G2
Levins Court 21 C3
Ley Brook 11 D3
Ley, The 15 D5
Lhen Close 7 B3
Library Steps (3) 25 D4
Lichfield Close 13 C4
Lidgates Green 11 A4
Lightmoor Road 20 F2
Lilac Close 11 D5
Lilac Meadows 15 A2
Lily Terrace 6 E5
Lilyhurst Road 8 E3
Lilyvale Close 13 B5
Lime Court*, Linden Way ..28 F2
Lime Grove 27 B4
Lime Tree Way 4 F6
Limekiln Bank 13 A3
Limekiln Close 13 A3
Limekiln Lane (Lilleshall)
.........................8 F5/H4/H5
Limekiln Lane (Wellington)
.....................10 F5/G3/G4
Limes Walk 12 F3
Limes, The 29 C3

Lincoln Crescent 12 F1
Lincoln Hill 20 E5/23 A1
Lincoln Road 12 F1
Lincoln Villas*, Woodland Road
....12 F1
Linden Avenue 10 E2
Linden Court*, Linden Way 28 F2
Linden Grove 10 E2
Linden Terrace 11 C5
Linden Way 28 F2
Lindens, The.....................18 G3
Lindfield Drive 10 E1
Lineton Close 6 F5
Linley Drive.......................16 G6
Linley House*, Victoria Road
....27 D3
Linley View Drive 25 B1
Linnet Gate 3 D4
Lintin Close 3 C4
Lion Lane 29 B5
Lion Street.........................12 F3
Listley Street 25 C3
Little Croft*, Oldcroft 12 E2
Little Eyton Fold 16 E3
Little Meadow Close 3 B5
Little Worth 19 B1
Llewellyn Roberts Way 28 F1
Lloyds Head 20 H6/23 D2
Lloyds Jitty*, Quarry Rd. ...23 A3
Lloyds Mount 20 G5/23 C1
Lloyds Road 20 G6
Lloyds, The ..20 G6/22 F5/23 C2
Loak Road 29 A2
Lodge Close 18 G4
Lodge Lane (Bridgnorth)
....26 E3/E4
Lodge Lane (Brosley) 23 A6
Lodge Lane (Ironbridge)
....20 F4/23 B1
Lodge Road (Donn. Wd.) 7 C6
Lodge Road (Donnington)
....6 H6/7 A6
Lodge Road (St. Georges) 12 H3
Lodgewood Lane 13 A3
London Road 12 H3
Long Croft.........................29 D2
Long End Drive 21 D1
Long Lane 20 G3
Long Lane Drive 20 G3
Long Meadow 16 H4
Longford Rise 4 F6
Longford Road 24 E4
Longford Turning 27 B3
Longford View 27 B3
Longlands Lane 28 F2
Longmynd Court*, Severn Drive
....3 D6
Longnor Road......................3 D6
Longslow Close 27 D2
Longslow Road 27 B1/C2/D3
Longthorpe Drive 5 A5
Lonsdale Court*, The Lawns
....28 F2

Lonsdale Court*, West Castle St. 25 D4
Lord Murray Drive 20 H2
Lords Drive 13 A2
Love Lane (Bridgnorth) 25 D2
Love Lane (Cleo. Mort.) 29 B5
Love Lane (Mkt. Dray.) 28 E3
Lovell Close 18 H2
Low Valley Close 11 B2
Lowe Court 10 F2
Lower Bar 24 F3
Lower Brook 11 D6
Lower Dingle 20 H5/23 D1
Lower Farm Cottages 3 A1
Lower Inhedge 29 D5
Lower Park Drive 3 D4
Lower Street 29 C5
Lower Wood 11 D6
Loweswater Close 12 H5
Lowry Close 3 D4
Lucerne Close 5 B6
Ludford Drive 16 G6
Ludlow Drive 16 F5
Ludlow Heights 25 B4
Ludlow Road (Bridgnorth) 25 A5/B3
Ludlow Road (Cleo. Mort.) 29 A6
Lychgate Walk*, King Street 10 F1
Lydbury Close 16 G6
Lyle Court 10 F1
Lyncroft 29 C3
Lyndhurst Drive 6 E5
Lytham Green 7 B3

M

Maddocks 21 A4
Maddocks Court 10 F2
Madebrook Close 21 D4
Madeley Road 20 F5/23 B1
Madeley Wood View 20 H5/23 D1
Maer Lane 28 E2
Mafeking Drive 12 G1
Mafeking Road 11 A1
Mafeking Terrace 12 G1
Magna Close 15 D5
Magnolia Drive 11 D5
Magpie Way 21 B1
Main Road 12 E4
Majestic Way 16 E6/20 H1
Malcolm Davies Drive 6 F6
Malinsgate 1 B4
Mall, The 26 E4
Mallard Close 21 D1
Malory Drive 16 E6
Malthouse Bank 19 B1
Maltings, The 10 E2
Malvern Crescent 15 D6
Manchester Drive 4 H4
Mannerley Lane (Ketley) ..11 D4
Mannerley Lane (Overdale) 11 D5

Manor Close (Mkt. Dray.) ..28 E3
Manor Close (Shifnal) 18 G4
Manor Cottages 14 G2
Manor Drive 12 G4
Manor Farm Cottages 25 B5
Manor Farm Lane 25 A6
Manor Gardens (Albrighton) 29 C3
Manor Gardens (Dawley) ..15 D5
Manor Gardens (Mkt. Dray.) 28 E3
Manor Heights 11 A1
Manor Rise 11 A3
Manor Road (Dawley) 15 D5
Manor Road (Hadley) 11 B1
Manor Road (Wellington) ..10 H3
Manse Close 11 B1
Manse Road 11 B1
Mansell Road 10 E2
Maple Close (Mkt. Dray.) ..27 B4
Maple Close (Shifnal) 18 G2
Maple Close (Trench) 6 E6
Maple Wood 16 H4
Marchwood Close 25 B1
Margaret Court 11 A2
Marigold Court 11 C4
Market Approach*, Market Street 10 E2
Market Arcade*, Market Street 10 E2
Market Drayton Bypass 27 A4/28 E1
Market Mews 24 F4
Market Place 18 G3
Market Square 10 F2
Market Street (Oakengates) 12 F3
Market Street (Wellington) 10 E2
Marlborough Road 11 C1
Marlborough Way 11 C5
Marley Mount Crescent 28 E2
Marlow Drive 6 F6
Marnwood Cottages 19 C3
Marquis Terrace 12 F4
Marrions Hill 12 G3
Marsh Meadow Close 3 D5
Marsh Road 14 H2
Marshbrook Way 7 A3/B4
Mart Avenue 12 H4
Martin Road 9 D1
Martingale Way 15 B1
Marton Drive 3 D6/10 E1
Masefield Close 27 C4
Mason Drive 21 A3
Masons Place 24 F2
Matlock Avenue 16 E3
Maudlins Close 25 B3
Maurice Lee Avenue 12 E2
Mawley Court 29 C4
Mayfair Close 29 C2
Mayfair Grove 13 B3
Mayfield 21 A4
Mayfield Road 29 C2

Maynards Croft 24 G2
Maypole Road 23 B3
Maythorne Close 21 C4
McCormick Drive 3 D4
McLean Drive 13 A4
Meadcroft 21 A3
Meadow Brook Close 21 B4
Meadow Close (Bridgnorth) 25 C4
Meadow Close (Madeley)..21 C4
Meadow Close (Mkt. Dray.)27 D2
Meadow Close (Trench) 5 D6
Meadow Dale Drive 3 B5
Meadow Drive 18 H1
Meadow Road (Albrighton)29 D3
Meadow Road (Dawley) ...15 D3
Meadow Road (Muxton) 7 A3
Meadow Road (Newport) ..24 G4
Meadow Road (Wellington) 9 D4
Meadow View Close 24 G3
Meadow View Road 24 G3
Meadowlea 21 B3
Meadows, The (Ketley Bank) 12 E4
Meadows, The (Lawley) ..15 A1
Meadowsweet Drive 13 A4
Meadway (Bridgnorth) 26 E4
Meadway (Shifnal) 18 H3
Medlar Close 11 D5
Meese Close 4 E6
Meeson Close 29 D3
Melbourne Close 16 E3
Mellor Close .....20 H5 /23 D1
Melrose Crescent 27 D4
Melrose Gardens 10 E2
Mendip Close 15 D6
Merchant Court*, Cheshire St. 28 E2
Mercia Drive 10 H1
Mercian Court (Mkt. Dray.) 28 E2
Mercian Court (Shifnal) ...18 G2
Mere Close (Newport) 24 F2
Mere Close (Shifnal) 18 H4
Mere Grove 3 D3
Meretown Road 24 H1
Merevale Way 7 A2
Merganser Close 4 G5
Merlin Coppice 4 H4
Merridale Crescent 10 F1
Merrington Road 7 B2
Merton Terrace 25 C5
Meyrick Road 4 E6
Middle Road 12 F1
Middle Street 22 G2
Midgley Court*, Lower Bar 24 F3
Midland Court 20 F3
Mill Bank 10 G2
Mill Farm Drive 16 H3
Mill Lane (Broseley) 23 A5
Mill Lane (Kemberton) 22 H4
Mill Lane (Madeley) 21 B4
Mill Lane (Wellington) 10 G2
Mill Pool Place*, Lower St. 29 C5

Mill Street 26 E3
Mill Terrace 6 F5
Mill Way 6 E5
Millers Green 29 C3
Millers Way 7 B3
Millfield Drive 28 G2
Millfields Road 10 G2
Millman Grove 15 B1
Millstream Way 5 A5/A6
Millward Close 6 G4
Milners Court 15 D1
Milners Lane 15 C2
Milton Drive (Ironbridge) 20 H4/21 A4
Milton Drive (Mkt. Dray.) ...28 E1
Mimosa Close 21 B5
Minchers Rise 11 C6
Miners Meadow 23 C5
Mines, The 23 A3
Minton Close 20 H2
Mitchel Way 21 A3
Moat Close 3 D5
Moat Croft 18 G4
Moat Street 25 D3
Mold Court 25 D2
Mole Way 3 D4
Monet Close 3 D4
Monks Court 26 E3
Monksfield 27 C2
Montgomery Mews 4 H4
Montgomery Road 9 D1
Moor Road 16 E3
Moorfield Lane 24 E4
Moorfields Court 24 E4
Moorhead 5 C1
Moorhouse Close 10 E2
Moorland Drive 13 A5
Moorland Road 24 E4
Morden Close 12 G3
Moreton Coppice 15 A4
Morfe Road 26 E4
Morgan Springs 25 C4
Morgan Way 11 B3
Morris Drive 6 H3
Mortimer Crescent 27 B6
Mortimer Gardens 29 B5
Mortimer Hill 29 C5
Mortimer Road 27 A6
Mortimer Terrace 29 C5
Morton Court 15 C3
Morville Drive 3 D5
Mosclay Road 12 H4
Moss Green Way 11 D3
Moss Road 6 G6/12 G1
Mossey Green 11 D4/12 E4
Mound Way 20 H4
Mount Gilbert 10 G4
Mount Lane 28 E3
Mount Pleasant 12 F4
Mount Pleasant Drive 21 B1
Mount Pleasant Road 21 C4
Mount Road 16 E3
Mount View Road 12 F4

Mountbatten Close **18** H1
Mounts Close **21** C4
Mountside **11** C4
Mulberry Close **24** F5
Mulberry Court **11** A1
Mullinder Drive **12** E5
Musk Rose Close **7** A4
Muxton Grange Cottages ...**7** C4
Muxton Lane **7** B2
Myford **15** A5
Myford Cottages*,
   Wellington Road **15** A5

N

Nabb Close......................**12** G3
Nabb, The **12** F2
Naird Farm Road **17** A2
Naird Lane....................**17** A5/B2
Nanny Murphys Lane*,
   Newport Road **18** H1
Near Vallens **11** C1
Nelson Court (Shifnal) **18** H1
Nelson Court (Wellington)..**10** F2
Nelson Way **7** B2
Nevil Road **9** D1
New Brookdale **11** A1
New Church Close **10** F2
New Church Road.............**10** F2
New Cottages **26** E1
New Hadley Villas.............**11** C1
New Hall Road **10** F2
New Houses **18** H3
New Inn Row*, Simon Evans Cl.
   ....**29** C5
New River Close................**3** D5
New Road (Bridgnorth)......**25** D4
New Road (Cleo. Mort.) **29** C5
New Road (Dawley) **15** D4
New Road (Donnington) **6** H4
New Road (Ironbridge)
   ....**20** E5/23 A1
New Road (Madeley) **21** A4
New Road (Wrkwdine. Wd.)
   ....**6** G6/12 F1
New Road Gardens **29** C5
New Row **1** C5
New Row (Horsehay) **15** B3
New Street (Centre) **1** D5
New Street (Dawley)..........**15** D4
New Street (Newport) **24** F4
New Street (Oakengates) ..**12** F3
New Street (St. Georges) ..**12** G3
New Street (Wellington) **10** F2
New Trench Road
   ....**5** D5/6 F4/7 A2/8 F5
New Works Lane **10** H6
Newbridge Road **20** G5/23 C1
Newcastle Road................**28** G2
Newcomen Way **20** F4
Newfield Close **18** G2
Newfield Court **6** E6
Newfield Drive...................**6** E6
Newhouse Lane **29** C3

Newill Grove **3** C4
Newlands Road..................**12** F4
Newport Bypass **24** G1/G6/H3
Newport Crescent.............**18** G2
Newport Road (Albrighton) **29** B1
Newport Road (Mkt. Dray.) **28** F3
Newport Road (Shifnal)
   ....**14** H6/18 H2
Newtonmere Drive **10** E1
Newtown (Dawley) **15** D3
Newtown (Mkt. Dray.) **28** E3
Newtown (Newport) **24** E6
Nickless Way **15** D2
Nightingale Way **4** G5
Norbroom Court **24** G3
Norbroom Drive **24** G3
Norfield View....................**16** H3
Norman Brook Court.........**28** E3
North Road **4** E6/10 E1
North Sherwood Street **1** D5
North Street **12** G3
North View Flats **18** H3
Northgate **25** D2
Northgate Mews*, Northgate
   ....**25** D2
Northwood Terrace **16** F4
Norton Drive **16** F6
Norwich Drive **16** H4

O

Oak Avenue **24** F5
Oak Close........................**21** C3
Oak Cottages **22** G2
Oak Gardens **25** B2
Oak Road **11** C5
Oak View*, Manor Gdns. ...**28** E3
Oakengates Road **6** G6
Oakfield Road (Mkt. Dray.) **27** D3
Oakfield Road (Shifnal) **18** G2
Oakfield Road (Telford) **3** D3
Oaklands (Bridgnorth).......**26** F4
Oaklands Drive **6** F5
Oaklands, The (Newport) ..**24** F5
Oaks Crescent **9** D3/D4
Oakwood Drive **6** E5
Okehampton Road **5** A5
Old Bakery Row*, The Parade
   ....**10** F2
Old Coppice Grange **12** E5
Old Dalelands*, Charlesway
   ....**27** D4
Old Farm Lane **8** H5
Old George Mews*, High Street
   ....**28** F3
Old Hall **7** D1/8 G6
Old Hall Close (Albrighton) **29** B3
Old Hall Close (Wellington) **10** G3
Old Incline **6** G6
Old Mill Lane....................**25** C5
Old Nursery Close.............**21** B3
Old Office Close **15** D2
Old Office Place **6** G6
Old Office Road **15** C2/C3

Old Park Road **12** F4
Old Park Way **11** D6
Old Smithfield **18** H3
Old Toll Gate **12** G2
Old Vicarage Road **15** D5
Old Wharf **16** E3
Old Whitchurch Road*,
   Severn Drive **3** D6
Old Willow Road **7** B2
Old Worcester Road **26** F5
Oldbury Road **25** B5/B6
Oldbury Terrace **25** C4
Oldbury Wells **25** C4
Oldcroft **12** E2
Oldfield Road **16** E5
Oleander Close.................**11** D5
Oliver Court......................**10** F1
Onny Grove **12** H1
Onslow Drive **3** D6
Orchard Close (Lit. Wen.) **19** B2
Orchard Close (Ketley) **11** B3
Orchard Close (Mkt. Dray.)**27** C3
Orchard Close (Newport) ..**24** F6
Orchard Drive **25** C2
Orchard End **29** B4
Orchard Lane **20** F5/23 B1
Orchard Rise....................**27** C3
Orchard Road **18** H2
Orchard Way **10** G2
Orchard, The **29** C3
Orchid Close **7** A4
Orient Court......................**20** F3
Orleton Lane **9** D1
Orleton Mews **9** D1
Orleton Terrace **10** E2
Ormsdale Close **7** A3
Osprey Grove **4** H4
Osterley Grove **7** B3
Ottley Way **27** B6
Oval Close **13** A3
Oval, The (Mkt. Dray.).......**28** E3
Oval, The (Newport) **24** G3
Overdale **11** C5
Owen Close **17** A5
Owen Terrace **23** A4
Oxford Road **16** E3
Oxford Street....................**12** F3
Oxlip Close **7** A4

P

Paddock Close **9** D1
Paddock Court **15** D4
Paddock Lane **22** G2
Paddock Mount................**15** D4
Paddock, The (Shifnal)......**18** G3
Paddocks, The (Cleo. Mort.)
   ....**29** B4
Paddocks, The (Mkt. Dray.)**27** D2
Paddocks, The (Muxton)......**7** B3
Paddocks, The*, Shepherds La.
   ....**11** C3
Padmans Alley **23** A4
Pageant Drive **16** E6

Pale Meadow Road **25** D4
Panorama **12** F2
Papermill Cottages **29** C4
Parade, The (Donnington) ..**6** G4
Parade, The (Shifnal) **18** H3
Parade, The (Wellington) ..**10** F2
Paradise **20** E5/23 A1
Pargeter Close **16** E6/21 B1
Parish Close **15** D5
Parish Drive **11** C1
Park Avenue **21** B4
Park Close **13** A3
Park Court (Shifnal) **18** G4
Park Court (Telford) **20** G3
Park End **24** F2
Park Lane (Centre) **1** A2
Park Lane (Madeley) **20** G3
Park Lane (Old Park) **20** G3
Park Lane (Shifnal)...........**18** H4
Park Lane Avenue ..**20** H4/21 A4
Park Road (Centre)............**1** A5
Park Road (Dawley Bank)
   ....**15** D1/D2
Park Road (Donnington)......**6** G5
Park Street (Madeley).......**21** A4
Park Street (Shifnal) **18** H4
Park Street (Wellington) **10** F1
Park View (Broseley) **23** B5
Park View*, Hadley Road. **12** E2
Parkdale **5** B6
Parker Bowles Drive **27** C3
Parklands **4** E6
Parkway **20** H4/21 A3
Partridge Close...................**4** G6
Parville House*, Vineyard Road
   ....**10** E1
Pasmore Close **21** A1
Pasteur Drive **4** G5
Patshull Road **29** B3
Paulbrook Road **25** C3
Pave Lane **24** G6
Pavilion Grove **13** A3
Pearson Road **12** G5
Pell Wall*, Newport Road ..**28** F3
Pemberton Road **3** B5/B6
Pembridge Close **6** H2
Pembroke Drive **10** G1
Pen y Bryn Way **24** F5
Pendil Close **9** D3
Pendrel Close **27** B6
Penistone Close **6** H5
Peregrine Way **4** G4
Perivale Gardens **7** B3
Perry Court **4** E6
Peters Close **15** D5
Peveril Bank **15** D2
Pezenas Drive **27** D2
Phoenix Bank **28** F3
Picasso Close **3** D4
Pickering Road **6** F6
Pickstock Close **16** G6
Pickthorn Court*,
   Maurice Lee Avenue ..**12** E2

Pickwick Court 18 H2
Picton Close 12 H2
Pine Close 27 D3
Pine View 7 A3
Pinefields 18 H3
Pineway 26 F3
Pinewood Avenue...............6 E5
Pinewoods 24 E6
Pinfold................................14 H1
Pinkham 29 C5
Pinkham Lane....................29 D5
Pintail Drive 4 G4
Pippins, The 16 H4
Pitchford Drive 13 B5
Pitchford Road 29 B3
Plant Close 15 C1
Plough Lane 24 G1
Plough Road (Wellington)..10 F1
Plough Road (Wrkwdine. Wd.)
....6 G6
Ploughmans Croft.............24 G3
Plover Gate.........................3 D4
Poachers Gate 15 D2
Police Drive.......................28 E3
Pond Street........................25 C3
Pool Close 5 D6
Pool Drive 25 C3
Pool Farm Avenue 4 H6
Pool Hill.............................15 C5
Pool Hill Road 15 B4
Pool Meadow 11 C1
Pool Road............................6 E6
Pool Side 15 B3
Pool View 15 B4
Pooler Close 10 E3
Poplar Close 21 C4
Poplar Drive 9 D1
Poppy Drive 7 A4
Porchester Close 5 A5
Port Way............................21 C3
Portia Close 9 D1
Portland Drive (Mkt. Dray.) 27 C3
Portland Drive (Telford) 11 D6
Portley Corner...................15 D4
Portley Road......................15 D4
Portmans Way 25 B3
Portobello Close 11 D5
Postern Gate 25 D3
Potters Bank 11 C3
Pound Lane 23 C6
Pound Street......................25 C3
Powder Lane 9 D2
Powell Place 24 F3
Powell Road 13 A4
Powis Drive........................10 E1
Powis Place 15 D2
Prestage Close 23 C6
Preston Grove......................6 E5
Preston Trust Homes 5 C1
Priestland Terrace 6 E4
Primmer Road......................4 H2
Primrose Drive 24 F6
Primrose Grove 10 G3

Prince Andrew Drive 16 E1
Prince Charles Crescent......1 A6
Prince Edward Crescent 16 E1
Prince Street (Madeley) 21 C3
Princes End 15 C1
Princes Street (Wellington)
....10 G3
Princess Anne Gardens 15 C4
Princess Avenue................10 H3
Princess Drive....................25 B2
Princess Gardens 24 F5
Priors Gate 13 A5
Priors Lane 27 C2
Priorslee Avenue 2 G1/13 B5
Priorslee Road
.................12 G4/H5/17 D1/18 E1
Priorslee Village 2 H1/H2
Priory Close (Bridgnorth) ..26 E4
Priory Close (Wellington) ..10 F3
Priory Court........................27 C2
Priory Road (Bridgnorth) ...26 E4
Priory Road (Telford) 12 E2
Pritchard House*, Church Street
....23 B5
Proctors Place 12 G1
Prospect Road (Mkt. Dray.)27 D2
Prospect Road (Wellington)
....10 G2
Pughs Jitty*, Quarry Rd. .. 23 A3
Punta Verde Drive 21 B5
Purbeck Dale 15 D3
Purcell Court*, Roseway 10 F2
Purton Wood View 16 H3

Quail Gate 3 D4
Quarry Bank Road 27 D4
Quarry House Lane 27 C4
Quarry Lane 11 D3
Quarry Place (Dawley) 15 C4
Quarry Place (Mkt. Dray.)..27 D4
Quarry Road 23 A3
Quarry, The 27 D5
Quayside 21 C3
Queen Elizabeth Avenue ..16 G2
Queen Elizabeth Way 1 A6
Queen Street (Broseley) ...23 A4
Queen Street (Madeley) ...21 C3
Queen Street (Mkt. Dray.)..28 E2
Queen Street (Wellington) 10 E1
Queens Court 21 C4
Queens Drive 24 F5
Queens Road (Bridgnorth)
.....................................26 E3/E4
Queens Road (Donnington) 6 H5
Queensway (Brookside)
.................................21 A1/D1
Queensway (Centre) ..1 D1/2 G4
Queensway (Dawley) 17 A3
Queensway (Hadley)......5 A4/C4
Queensway (Leegomery) 4 E4
Queensway (Oakengates) 12 E1
Queensway Drive 25 B2

Queenswood Close...........12 F5
Quines Close 7 A3
Quorn Grove 27 C3

R

Racecourse Drive 25 B3
Radnor Court 10 H1
Ragged Robins Close........12 H2
Railway Street....................25 D3
Ralph Jones Terrace*,
     Ludlow Road 29 A6
Rampart Way 1 D2
Ramshurst Court*,
     Kensington Way 12 F3
Randlay Avenue 16 G3/H4
Randlay Centre 16 G3
Randlay Fields 16 H4
Raven Court 28 E2
Ravenhill Drive 12 E5
Ravensdale Drive 7 A3
Rea Drive 4 E6
Rectory Road 29 B2
Red Bank 27 D4
Red Bank Crescent 27 D3
Red Bank Lane 27 D4
Red Bank Road 27 D4
Red Church Close 23 C3
Red Hill Way 13 A1
Red House Bungalows*,
     High Street 29 C2
Red House Flats*, High St.29 C2
Red House*, Shropshire Street
....28 E3
Red Kite Close 4 H6
Red Lake 11 D4
Red Lees.....................11 B3/C3
Redburn Close 12 E4
Redchurch Close 23 C3
Redfield Close 23 C3
Redford Drive 29 D2
Redlands Road..................11 C1
Rednall Fields 15 D6
Redthorne Hill...................29 C6
Redwing Close 4 G6
Redwood Close 3 C3
Reed Close........................12 G2
Regal Court*, Gladstone Street
....11 B1
Regent Drive 12 G3
Regent Square 21 B3
Regent Street 10 G2
Rembrandt Drive.................3 C4
Rendal Court*, Ironmasters Way
....12 G6
Reynards Coppice 21 B6
Reynards Meadow 21 B5
Reynolds Drive 12 F3
Reynolds Wharf 22 G6
Rhodes Avenue 16 E2
Richards House*, Richards Rd.
....6 H1
Richards Road 6 H1
Richmond Avenue 6 E6

Richmond Close 24 F6
Richmond Court 4 F6
Richmond Gardens...........25 C2
Riddings Close (Broseley) 23 C6
Riddings Close (Ketley) 11 C4
Ridings Close (Mkt. Dray.) 27 D2
Ridley Close 25 B3
Ringers Way 3 B5
Ripley Close 5 A6
Riven Road 11 C1
River View*, Hospital St. 26 E4
Riverside............................25 D3
Riverside Avenue 22 H6
Riverside Caravan Park 25 D5
Robert Moore Flats *, Church St.
....21 B4
Roberts Drive 15 B2
Roberts Road 20 G4
Robins Drive......................20 G3
Rochester Close 16 H4
Rock Acres 8 G6
Rock Road 11 B4
Rock Terrace 12 H3
Rock, The (Sheriff.)...........14 H2
Rock, The (Telford)...........11 C6
Rockall Way 11 D6
Rockfield Terrace 12 F2
Rockley Bank 29 C5
Roddam Court....................24 F4
Roden Close 4 E6
Rodenhurst House*,
     Cheshire Street 28 E2
Rodney Close 18 H2
Roe Deer Green 24 F1
Roman Grove 12 G3
Roman Road.......................9 A3
Ronhill Crescent 29 B5
Ronhill Lane 29 C4
Rookery Road....................12 H2
Rookery, The (Madeley) 21 B4
Rookery, The (St. Georges)
....12 H2
Rope Walk 19 D2
Rose Crescent 10 F3
Rose Lane 25 C3
Rose Tree Close................11 D5
Rosegrove..........................10 F3
Rosehill Drive 25 C3
Roseway 10 F2
Roslyn Road 10 F1
Rosthwaite 10 F3
Rothesay Grove 12 E5
Rothwell Close 12 H3
Rough Lane 23 D6
Round Oak Drive 4 E5
Roundhouse Park 15 A6
Row, The 22 H4
Rowallan Way 13 B4
Rowan Avenue 16 E5
Rowan Drive 24 F5
Rowan Road 28 F1/F2
Rowland Gate 10 E2
Rowley Close 20 H5/23 D1

Rowton Close 4 F6
Royal Oak Drive 4 H5
Ruith Field.......................3 C3
Rush Lane 27 C1
Rushbury Road...................3 D6
Rushmoor Lane 3 A2
Ruskin Way......................16 E6
Russell Close 26 H4
Russell Road 21 B3
Russell Square 21 B4
Russells, The 18 G3
Rutland Green 10 H1
Ryder Drive........................7 B4
Ryebank Road 12 E5
Ryelands Gardens 25 B3
Rylands 24 F2
Ryton Way 16 F6

S

Sabrina Road 25 D4
Sadlers Fold 12 E5
Saggars Close 20 H5/23 D1
Salisbury Avenue 13 C4
Salisbury Hill View 27 D4
Salisbury Road 27 C4/D4
Salop Street 25 C3
Salters Court*, Lower Bar ..24 F3
Salters Lane 24 E4
Salters Mews*, Salters La. 24 E4
Salthouse Road
.................20 H6/22 F5/23 D2
Saltwells Drive 7 A3
Sambrook Close...............16 G6
Sambrook Crescent 28 G1
Sandal Close 5 A5
Sandbrook 11 B2
Sandcroft 21 D5
Sanderstead Court 11 A1
Sanderville Close 16 H6
Sandiford Crescent 24 E4
Sandino Court...................16 H6
Sandpiper Close.................4 G6
Sandringham Close 28 F1
Sandway 11 A2
Sandy Croft 24 F3
Sandy Lane (Albrighton) 29 B1
Sandy Lane (Mkt. Dray.)
.............................28 E4/F6
Saplings, The 20 F3
Savannahs, The 4 E5
Saville Close 10 E2
Saxon Court 4 H5
Sceptre Close 20 H1
School Close 18 G4
School Cottages 19 B1
School Court.....................10 G2
School Grove 12 E3
School Grove Lane............24 G3
School Lane (Ketley) 11 C3
School Lane (Mkt. Dray.) ..27 C4
School Lane (Wellington) ..10 G3
School Road (Coalbrkdale.)
...............................20 E3

School Road (Donnington)
..............................6 H3/H4
School Road (Madeley) 20 G4
School Street 12 H3
Scott Close 21 C5
Second Avenue................12 F4
Selbourne 21 C5
Selkirk Drive 21 D5
Seven Hills Place 11 B3
Severn Bank...........20 E5/23 A1
Severn Drive 4 E5/E6
Severn Gorge Camping &
Caravan Park 21 C2
Severn Street 25 D4
Severn Terrace (Ironbridge)
...............................22 F5
Severn Terrace (Quatford) 26 H6
Severn Terrace*, Bandon Lane
...............................26 E3
Severn Valley Way ..19 D5/20 F6
Severn Walk 21 C5
Severn Way 15 D6
Severnside 20 F6/23 B2
Severnside South 25 D3
Shaftsbury Close 13 B3
Shakespeare Way 21 C6
Shambles*, High Street......28 F3
Shamrock Way 16 H4
Sharp Close 3 B5
Shaw Croft 14 H1
Shaw Lane (Albrighton) 29 D2
Shaw Lane (Shifnal) 17 C4
Shawbirch Cottages 4 F4
Shawbirch Road 3 C5
Shawfield Close 21 C5
Sheepwell Court 12 E5
Sheldon Court..................29 C3
Shellduck Drive 4 G5
Shelley Drive...................21 C6
Shelsey Court 21 B3
Shepherds Court 24 G3
Shepherds Fold 15 D2
Shepherds Lane 11 C3
Sherbourne Close............12 H1
Sheridan Way 21 D5
Sheriffhales Drive 14 G1
Sherlock Hoy Close 23 B5
Sherwood Close 3 D3
Sherwood Crescent 27 B4
Sherwood Row 1 D5
Sherwood Square 1 D5
Sherwood Street................1 D5
Shetland Close 15 B5
Shifnal Cottages 18 G4
Shifnal Road 2 G1/13 A6
Shipton Close 16 G6
Shirefields Way 15 B4
Shires, The 2 H2
Shop Cottages 8 H3
Shoveller Drive 4 G5
Shrewsbury Fields 18 G3
Shrewsbury Road (Shifnal)
...............................18 G3

Shrewsbury Road (Mkt. Dray.)
............................27 A4/D3
Shrewsbury Way 24 E4
Shropshire Street 28 E3
Shrubbery Road 11 D4
Shuker Close 24 G4
Shutfield Road 21 A1
Sidbury Close 16 G5
Sidings, The*, Frogmore Road
...............................28 E2
Silkin View......................16 F5
Silkin Way 5 C4
Silverbirch Grove 7 A3
Silverdale Close 24 E5
Silverdale Paddocks 3 B5
Silvermere......................13 A4
Silvermere Mews 18 H4
Silvermere Park 18 H4
Silvington Close 16 G6
Simon Close 10 E2
Simon Evans Close 29 C5
Simons Road 27 D3
Simpsons Lane 23 A3
Simpsons Walk 15 A4
Sinclair Gardens 11 B4
Sinclair Grove 11 B3
Singleton.........................21 D4
Sixth Avenue...................12 F5
Slaney Court*, Slaney Street
...............................12 F3
Slaney Street 12 F3
Smallbrook 11 D6
Smallwood 21 C5
Smallwood Court..............24 F4
Smarts Way 12 H2
Smith Crescent..................6 G6
Smithfield Close 28 F2
Smithfield Road 28 E2/F2
Smithy Bank 23 B5
Snedshill Way 12 H5
Snow Hill.........................12 H3
Snowdrop Meadow...........11 C3
Snows Court 24 F4
Solway Drive....................21 D5
Somerset Close 20 H5/23 D1
Sommerfeld Road 5 C6/11 D1
Songthrush Close...............4 G6
Sorrel Close 7 A4
South Drive 21 A4
South View (Donnington) 6 H5
South View (Trench Lock) ..5 C6
South View (Wrockwardine) 9 A1
South View Drive 15 D6
South View Road 15 D6
Southall..........................16 E6
Southall Road 16 E5/E6
Southfield 21 C6
Southgate 21 B5
Southorn Court 23 A3
Southwater 1 D5
Southwater Arcade 1 C6
Southwater Way 1 B5
Southwell Close 13 C4

Sovereign Close 20 H1
Spa Crescent 3 C5
Spafield Close 3 C4
Spanmeadow 3 D3
Sparrowhawk Way 4 G4
Speeds Lane.....................23 A4
Speedwell Ridge..............16 H4
Spencer Court 18 G3
Spencer Drive..................21 C6
Spinners Court 3 C3
Spinney, The (Muxton) 7 B3
Spinney, The (Newport) 24 F6
Spout Lane (Centre) 1 B6
Spout Lane (Lit. Wen.)......19 A1
Spout Lane (Broseley) 23 A3
Spout Way 16 F3
Spring Court 21 A4
Spring Hill (Mkt. Dray.) 28 E3
Spring Hill (Wellington) 10 E1
Spring Terrace (The Rock) 11 C5
Spring Terrace (Trench) 6 G5
Spring Village 15 B4
Springfield (Bridgnorth)......26 E4
Springfield Avenue 24 F5
Springfield Close 15 D4
Springfield Cottages 27 C3
Springfield Court 15 D4
Springfield Park 27 C3
Springfield Road 6 E5
Springfields (Newport).......24 F5
Springhill (Dawley) 15 C4
Springhill Close................21 C4
Springhill Crescent 21 C4
Springhill Road 15 C3
Springmeadow 21 C5
Spruce Drive......................4 H5
Square, The (Broseley).......23 B5
Square, The (Hadley) 11 B1
Square, The (Ironbridge)
...........................20 F2/23 B1
Square, The (Newport) 24 F4
Square, The (St. Georges)
...............................12 H3
Squires Close..........20 H5/23 D1
Squirrel Court 25 C3
Squirrel Meadow.................3 C4
St. Agathas Close 4 E4
St. Andrews Close 18 H2
St. Andrews Way 24 E6/F6
St. Aubin Drive 15 D1
St. Brelade Close 15 D1
St. Catherines Close...........4 F5
St. Chads Close 4 E6/10 E1
St. Christopher Way 15 D2
St. Cuthberts Crescent 29 B2
St. Davids Close 16 E1
St. Georges Road
.......................6 H5/H6/12 H1
St. Giles Close 10 G3
St. Helens Close 4 F5
St. Helier Drive.................15 C1
St. James Court 10 E2
St. James Crescent..........16 F6

St. James Drive 26 E4
St. John Street 10 F2
St. Johns Court 26 E3
St. Johns Drive 6 F6
St. Johns Street 26 E3
St. Julians Close 4 E5
St. Lawrence Close.............4 F5
St. Leonards Close 25 D3
St. Leonards Place 16 E2
St. Leonards Road 16 E2
St. Leonards Steps 25 D3
St. Leonards View 25 D2
St. Lukes Road (Doseley)..15 C5
St. Lukes Road (Ironbridge)
...............20 F5/23 B1
St. Margarets Drive 4 F6
St. Marks Close..................4 E4
St. Marks Drive 4 F5
St. Mary Street 24 F3
St. Marys Buildings*, High St.
...............28 F3
St. Marys Close (Albrighton)
...............29 C2
St. Marys Close (Broseley) 23 C3
St. Marys Court..................25 D3
St. Marys Place.................29 B5
St. Marys Steps (4)...........25 D4
St. Marys Street (Bridgnorth)
...............25 C3
St. Marys Street (Mkt. Dray.)
...............28 E3
St. Matthews Road......6 H5/7 A5
St. Michaels Close (Lilleshall)
...............8 G5
St. Michaels Close (Madeley)
...............21 B4
St. Michaels Drive 6 F6
St. Michaels Road.............21 B4
St. Michaels Walk 21 B4
St. Nicholas Crescent 26 E4
St. Nicholas Road 26 E4
St. Pauls Close 4 E5
St. Pauls Drive 4 F5
St. Peters Walk 3 B5
St. Quentins Gate 1 D6
St. Saviour Close 15 C1
St. Stephens Place 25 D4
Stable Lane 27 D2
Stables, The 7 B3
Stableyard Court...............15 B1
Stadium Way 11 B1
Stafford Avenue 18 G4
Stafford Court 2 G3
Stafford Park 1 ....2 H4
Stafford Park 2 ....2 G4
Stafford Park 4 ....17 B1
Stafford Park 5 ....17 B1
Stafford Park 6 ..13 B6/17 B1/C1
Stafford Park 7 ....2 H3/13 B6
Stafford Park 8 ....13 B6
Stafford Park 9 ....17 A1
Stafford Park 10 ....17 B1
Stafford Park 11 ....17 B1

Stafford Park 12 ....17 B2
Stafford Park 13 ....17 A1
Stafford Park 15 ....2 G5
Stafford Park 16 ....17 A2
Stafford Park 17 ....17 A2
Stafford Park 18 ....17 A1
Stafford Park Road 2 F3
Stafford Park Way.............17 A4
Stafford Place*, The Grove
...............18 H4
Stafford Road (Newport) 24 F3
Stafford Road (Oakengates)
...............12 F2
Stafford Street (Mkt. Dray.) 28 F2
Stafford Street (Newport) ..24 F4
Stafford Street (St. Georges)
...............12 G4
Stallard Court 12 E3
Stanall Drive 7 A3
Stanford Court...................10 F2
Stanier Drive 20 F3
Stanley Lane.....................25 D2
Stanley Lane Cottages 26 E1
Stanley Road 10 G2
Stanmore Cottages 26 H4
Stanmore Drive 6 E5
Stanton Road 18 H3
Stanwyke 21 D4
Station Approach (Bridgnorth)
...............25 D4
Station Approach (Newport)
...............24 G5
Station Court 24 F5
Station Fields 12 F3
Station Hill.........................12 F3
Station Lane 25 D4
Station Road (Admaston) 3 B5
Station Road (Albrighton) ..29 C2
Station Road (Cleo. Mort.) 29 C5
Station Road (Coalbrkdale.)
...............19 D4
Station Road (Dawley) 15 B4/C4
Station Road (Donnington)..6 G1
Station Road (Ketley) 11 B3
Station Road (Lawley Bank)
...............15 B1
Station Road (Madeley) 21 B4
Station Road (Newport)......24 F5
Station Road (Oakengates)
...............12 F3
Station Road (Wellington) ..10 F2
Station Terrace (Newport)..24 F5
Station Terrace*, Station Road
...............21 B4
Stebbings 21 D4
Steeple Close 29 B5
Steventon Road 9 D2
Stewardstone Gate 13 B4
Stewart Road 26 H3
Stile Rise 3 D4
Stirchley Avenue 16 G2/17 A4
Stirchley Hall Court 16 E5
Stirchley Lane 16 E5

Stirchley Road 16 F5/F6
Stirling Drive 21 C6
Stockford Close 13 B4
Stocking, The 20 F1
Stockton Close 16 G6
Stokes Road 27 A6
Stokesay Fore 21 C6
Stokesay Green 21 C6
Stokesay Link 21 C6
Stokesay Road 3 D5
Stokesay Way....................21 C6
Stone Crescent..................10 H3
Stone Row 16 E2
Stonebridge Close 21 A1
Stonechat Close 4 G6
Stonedale 21 C5
Stoneleigh Grove 7 B4
Stoneway Steps (5) 25 D3
Stoney Hill..........................20 E1
Stour Walk 12 H1
Stourbridge Road 26 E4/F5
Stowe Close 16 G6
Stratford Park 6 F4
Strethill Road 19 D3/D4/23 B2
Stretton Avenue 24 E4
Stretton Close (Bridgnorth) 25 B4
Stretton Close (Sutton Hill) 21 C6
Strine Close 4 E6
Strine Way 24 F2
Stuart Way 27 D1
Suffolk Way........................15 B4
Sulby Drive 4 G6
Summer Crescent..............12 G1
Summer House Drive 11 A1
Summerhill (Mkt. Dray.) 27 D4
Summerhill (Sutton Hill) 21 C5
Summerhill Gardens..........27 D4
Summerhouse Grove 24 G3
Sunbury Drive 6 F6
Sunderland Drive 4 H5
Sunflower Close 11 D4
Sunningdale 11 B1
Sunniside Avenue 19 D2
Sunny Gardens 24 F1
Sunnymead 21 C5
Sunnyside Road 11 D4
Sutherland Avenue 10 G1
Sutherland Drive 7 B2
Sutherland Road 10 G1
Sutherlands, The 7 A3
Sutton Bank 22 H6
Sutton Lane 27 D6
Sutton Road 3 B5
Sutton Way (Mkt. Dray.) 27 D4
Sutton Way (Telford) 21 B5/C6
Swallowfield Close 13 B4
Swan Gate 3 D4
Swan Street 23 B5
Swancote 26 H1
Swanmere 24 G1
Swansmede Way 16 G5
Sweet Briar Close 7 A3
Sweet Chestnut Grove 11 D6

Swift Gate 3 D4
Swinburne Close 21 C6
Swindon Drive 21 C6
Sycamore Close (Shifnal)..18 G2
Sycamore Close (Wellington)
...............9 D1
Sycamore Road 23 A3
Sycamore Terrace 16 E4
Sycamore Way 28 F1
Sydney Cottage Drive.......25 B2
Sylvan Close........................8 H3

T

Tadorna Drive....................16 H6
Talbot Close (Newport)......24 E5
Talbot Close (Shifnal).........18 G3
Talbot Close (Wrockwardine)
...............6 G6
Talbot Road (Albrighton)
...............29 B2/B3
Talbot Road (Trench) 6 G6
Talbot Square 29 B5
Talbot Villas*, Gower St.....12 H2
Tallis Court*, Roseway 10 F2
Tamarisk Close..................11 D5
Tan Bank (Newport) 24 F3
Tan Bank (Wellington)........10 F2
Tan Bank Mews*, Tan Bank
...............24 F3
Tanglewood Close 18 G4
Tarbach Close 23 C6
Tasley Close 25 B2
Tayleur Drive.....................27 B5
Teagues Crescent 6 E6
Teal Close 21 D1
Teawell Close 11 C6
Tee Lake Boulevard 3 D3/D4
Teece Drive 13 B5
Telford Avenue 29 D2
Telford Road (Bridgnorth) ..26 E2
Telford Road (Wellington)..10 E3
Telford Shopping Centre 1 D4
Telford Square 1 B4
Telford Way 2 F3/12 H6/13 A3
Teme Avenue 3 D5
Ten Tree Croft 10 E1
Tenbury Drive 6 F5
Tenbury Mead...................29 B6
Tenbury Road....................29 B6
Tennyson Close 27 C4
Teresa Way 4 G5
Tern Close 15 D6
Tern Hill Road....................27 A5
Tern Ridge 28 F3
Tern View 27 D5
Tern Way 4 E6
Thetford Chase 1 D5
Third Avenue 1 C1
Thirlmere Grove 12 H4
Thistle Close......................16 H4
Thornhill Court 28 E2
Thornton Park Avenue 7 B3
Three Ashes Road 25 B3

Timbers, The.....

Timbers, The.....................12 H2
Tining Close 25 B3
Toll Road 10 H4
Tom Morgan Close 15 B1
Tom Wedge Court 23 B6
Tompkinson Close 24 G2
Tontine Hill 20 E5/23 A1
Tow Row...........................22 H4
Tower Close 27 D2
Towers Lawn 28 E2
Town Walls 24 F5
Townsend Croft 6 H3
Trafalgar Close 7 A2
Trench Close 5 D5
Trench Lock 5 C6/11 D1
Trench Road 5 D6/6 E5
Trenleigh Gardens 6 E6
Trevithick Close*, Woodside
....20 E3
Trinity Place 15 D5
Trinity Road 15 D5
Trinity View 12 E4
Troon Way 21 C6
Tuckers Place 24 F4
Tuckies Hill 22 F6
Tuckies, The 22 F6
Tudor Close (Markrt Drayton)
....28 E1
Tudor Close (Newport)......24 G3
Tudor Meadow 5 D6
Tudor Way 18 H3
Tunnel Cottages 15 B2
Turberville Close...............12 H2
Turnpike Court 12 H3
Turnstone Drive 4 H6
Turreff Avenue 6 H3/H4
Turreff Bungalows...............9 A1
Tweedale Court 21 C2
Tweedale Crescent............21 C3
Tweedale North 21 C2
Tweedale South 21 C3
Tweedale Wharf 21 C3
Tynsley Court 21 B4
Tynsley Terrace 21 B4
Tyrley Road 28 H6

U

Ullswater Close.................12 H5
Underhill Close 24 F4
Underhill Street.................25 D4
Undertrees Close 4 E5
Underwood 23 B4
Union Court 11 C1
Union Road (Wellington)....10 E3
Union Road (Wrkwdine. Wd.)
....12 F1
Union Street 11 C1
Uplands Avenue 12 E2
Uplands Drive 25 B4
Upper Bar 24 F4
Upper Croft 23 B5
Upper Dingle 20 H5/23 D1
Upper Pool Hill 15 C4

Upper Road 21 A4
Upper Severn Terrace
.........................20 E5/23 A1
Upper Wood 11 D6
Upton Court*, The Lawns ..28 F2
Urban Gardens.................10 G2
Urban Road.......................12 F1
Urban Terrace 12 G2
Urban Villas 12 H2
Urban Way 10 G2

V

Valentino Row 20 F6/23 B2
Valley Court 25 C3
Valley Road (Overdale) 11 C5
Valley Road (Wellington) ..10 H4
Valley View 27 C4
Vaughan Road 29 B6
Vauxhall 24 E4
Vauxhall Crescent............24 E4
Vauxhall Terrace...............24 E4
Verbena Way 21 B6
Vernon Drive.....................27 D1
Vicar Street 12 E3
Vicarage Drive 18 G4
Vicarage Grove.................15 C4
Victoria Avenue (Ketley) ...11 B2
Victoria Avenue (Wellington)
....10 F2
Victoria Court (Hadley) 11 B1/C1
Victoria Court (Mkt. Dray.) 27 D3
Victoria Court (Shifnal) 18 G3
Victoria Court*, Victoria Road
....27 D3
Victoria Mews 10 F2
Victoria Mill 27 D4
Victoria Park 24 F3
Victoria Road (Bridgnorth) 25 B2
Victoria Road (Madeley) ...21 A3
Victoria Road (Mkt. Dray.) 27 D3
Victoria Road (Shifnal) 18 G3
Victoria Road (Wellington) 10 F2
Viewlands Drive 6 F5
Villa Court 21 B3
Village Close.....................12 E2
Village Court 2 H1
Village Way.......................12 E2
Villas, The 21 A6
Vineyard Court 24 G3
Vineyard Drive (Newport) ..24 F3
Vineyard Drive (Wellington)
....10 E1
Vineyard Place 10 E1
Vineyard Road (Newport) ..24 F3
Vineyard Road (Wellington)
....10 E1
Violet Close........................7 A4
Viols Walk 29 B5
Viscount Avenue...............21 A1

W

Wade Road 6 G6
Wadham Close....................4 G6

Waggoners Fold 16 E2
Wagtail Drive.....................21 A1
Wains Close 11 C6
Walder Close 15 C3
Walker Close.....................26 E4
Walker Crescent...............12 G2
Walker Street 10 E2
Walkmill Drive 28 E4
Walkmill Road...................28 E4
Wallshead Way 24 F6
Walnut Close (Newport) ...24 F5
Walnut Close (Telford) 21 A1
Walsh Close 13 B4
Walton Court*, Maurice Lee Av.
....12 E2
Waltondale 20 H3
Wantage 20 H3
Wardle Close 26 E4
Warren Court 28 E3
Warrensway 20 G4
Warwick Close 28 F1
Warwick Way 5 A5
Washbrook Road 25 D4
Water Lane 24 F3
Waterford Drive.................24 E5
Waterloo Bridge 11 B1
Waterloo Close 11 B1
Waterloo Road (Ketley)
.................................11 B1/B3
Waterloo Road (Wellington)
....10 F2
Waterloo Street........20 F6/23 B2
Waterloo Terrace*, Cartway
....25 D3
Waterlow Close.................13 C4
Waterside Drive 28 G1
Waterside Mews 24 E3
Watling Street (Red Hill)
.............................13 B3/14 E3
Watling Street (Wellington)10 G3
Waverley 21 A3
Wavertree Close...............12 G3
Waxhill Close 7 A5
Wayside 20 H3
Wealdstone 20 G3
Weavers Court 12 E4
Weavers Rise 12 E4
Webb Crescent.................15 C5
Wedgewood Crescent 11 A2
Weir Gardens 5 B6
Wellington Court Home 10 E3
Wellington Road (Lit. Wen.)
....19 A1
Wellington Road (Admaston)
....3 C5
Wellington Road (Coalbrkdale.)
....20 E3
Wellington Road (Donnington)
.............................6 G4/7 A2
Wellington Road (Horsehay)
.................................15 A2/A6
Wellington Road (Lilleshall)
.................................8 F6/H3

Wellington Road (Newport)
.............................24 E6/F5
Wellington Terrace 25 D3
Wellmeadow...........25 D4/26 E4
Wells Close.......................25 C3
Wells Place 29 C5
Wellsfield 21 A3
Wellswood Avenue 1 C1
Wenlock Drive...................24 F5
Wenlock Road 25 A3
Wensley Green.................20 H3
Wentworth Drive 20 H1
Wesley Crescent 18 G4
Wesley Drive.....................12 E4
Wesley Road 20 G5/23 C1
West Avenue 6 G5
West Castle Street 25 D4
West Centre Way 1 A5/15 B2
West End Terrace.............29 A6
West Road (Ketley Bank) ..12 E4
West Road (Wellington) 9 D2
West Street.......................12 G3
West View (Admaston) 3 B4
West View (Horsehay) 15 B4
West View Terrace 20 H4
Westbourne 20 G4
Westcroft Walk 13 A4
Westerdale Close 15 C5
Westerkirk Drive 20 H4
Western Rise 11 A2
Westfield Terrace 24 F4
Westgate 25 C3
Westgate Drive 25 B3
Westgate Villas*, Westgate
....25 C3
Westland Drive 25 B3
Westland Road 27 D3
Westlands, The...................7 B2
Westminster Drive 27 C4
Westminster Way 13 B4
Westmorland Mews 10 H1
Weston Close 18 H1
Weston Drive 9 D1
Weston Road 29 D2
Weybourne Walk 7 B4
Weybridge 20 G3
Weyman Road 4 E6
Wharf Close 12 G2
Wharfage Steps 20 E5
Wharfage, The 19 D5/23 A1
Wharfdale Cottages 28 G2
Wheat Leasows 5 B2
Wheatfield Drive 18 G2
Wheatlands Rise...............25 B3
Wheatlands, The...............25 B3
Wheatley Crescent 5 A5
Wheeldale Close 15 C5
Whimbrel Close 4 H6
Whiston Close 29 C3
Whitburn Street.................25 C3
Whitchurch Road 4 E5/F5
White Horse Close 15 D3
White Row 5 D2

Whitebeam Close 11 D5
Whitechapel Way 2 G2
Whitehall Gardens 23 B5
Whiteladies Court 29 B2
Whitemere Road...............10 E1
Whiteways Drive 3 B4
Whitmore Close (Bridgnorth)
....25 B1
Whitmore Close (Broseley)23 C6
Whitworth Drive 16 G4
Whyle Court*, Baldwin Webb Av.
....6 H4
Wicket Close.....................13 A3
Widewaters Close.............20 H1
Widgeon Grove 4 G5
Wigmores 21 A3
Wild Thyme Drive 7 A4
Wildwood 20 H3
Wilfred Owen Close 27 C4
Wilkinson Avenue 23 B5
Wilkinson Walk*, Cheshire St.
....28 E2
Willetts Way 15 C3
Williams Road.....................6 H1
Willmore Lane.....................8 H5
Willow Bank 21 A1
Willow Close 27 B4
Willow Court*, Turreff Avenue
....6 H4
Willowdale 18 G2
Willowfield 20 H3/21 A2
Willows Road 12 G2
Winchat Close 4 G6
Winchester Drive.................7 B4
Windermere Drive.............12 H5
Windmill Lane 29 A3
Windsor Crescent 23 B4
Windsor Drive 28 G1
Windsor Flats*, Windsor Road
....10 H3
Windsor Place 15 D4
Windsor Road (Albrighton) 29 C2
Windsor Road (Dawley) ...15 D4
Windsor Road (Wellington)10 H3
Winifreds Drive 6 G4
Winston Drive 6 H3
Witchwell Lane 19 A2
Withington Close 12 F2
Withybrook 20 G3
Withywood Drive.................1 B6
Wolverhampton Road
(Bridgnorth) 26 E3
Wolverhampton Road (Shifnal)
....18 H4
Wolverley Court 29 C3
Wombridge Road (Oakengates)
....................................12 E1/E2
Wombridge Road (Trench) ..6 E5
Wombridge Way 11 D3
Wood Close 6 G6
Woodberry Close....25 B2/B3
Woodbine Drive 7 A4
Woodcroft 20 H3

Woodford Green 3 C3
Woodhall Close 3 C4
Woodhouse Central 1 C4
Woodhouse Crescent 6 F5
Woodhouse Lane (Horsehay)
....15 A5
Woodhouse Lane (Priorslee)
....13 A4
Woodhouse Lane (Red Hill)
....13 D1
Woodhouse Road 23 B5
Woodland Close 29 C2
Woodland Road 12 F1
Woodland Villas 12 G1
Woodlands (Ironbridge)......20 F5
Woodlands Avenue 9 D2
Woodlands Close 23 B3
Woodlands Drive*,
The Woodlands 12 F1
Woodlands Green.............23 B3
Woodlands Lane 15 A5
Woodlands Rise 29 C4
Woodlands Road 20 F5/23 B1
Woodlands Road (Broseley)
....23 A3
Woodlands, The
(Wrkwdine. Wd.) 12 F1
Woodlands, The (Lilleshall) 8 H3
Woodlands, The (Red Lake)
....11 D4
Woodpecker Close 5 A4
Woodrows...........................20 H3
Woodrush Heath................11 D6
Woodside 20 E3
Woodside Avenue 20 F3/F4
Woodside Close 11 C3
Woodside Road 11 H3
Woodside Shops*, Park Lane
....20 H3
Woodside*, Barrack Lane...8 H3
Woodspring Grove 7 B4
Woodwell 11 D3
Woollam Road 10 H3
Woolpack Close 18 G2
Worcester Road 15 D3
Wordsworth Drive 27 C4
Wordsworth Way 12 H4
Worfe Close 16 H3
Worfe Road 18 G1
Worthington Drive 29 B2
Wrekin Avenue 24 E5
Wrekin Close......................6 E5
Wrekin Course 9 A6
Wrekin Drive.......................6 G4
Wrekin Home 10 E3
Wrekin Road (Bridgnorth) .25 B2
Wrekin Road (Wellington)..10 E2
Wrekin Square 1 C5
Wrekin Terrace*, Wellington Rd.
Wrekin View (Madeley)20 G4/G5
Wrekin View (Wrkwdine.) ...9 A1
Wrekin Walk 1 C5

Wrens Nest Lane 11 B4
Wrockwardine Road 9 C1
Wrockwardine Wood Way
...................................6 G6/12 E1
Wroxeter Way....................16 H6
Wych Elm Drive 4 E4
Wyke Place.......................18 H3
Wyke Rise 4 G6
Wyke Way.........................18 F3
Wyndham Grove................13 B3
Wynns Coppice*, Stoney Hill
....20 E1
Wyre Hall 1 C5
Wyvern 20 G4

Y

Yards, The 25 C3
Yates Way 1 B1
Yellowstone Close 12 H2
Yew Tree Court..................18 H3
Yew Tree Drive...........7 C1/8 F6
Yew Tree Road 20 H5/23 D1
York Flats*, High Street......10 F2
York Road..........................13 C4

HOSPITALS

Bridgnorth Hospital 25 C3
Princess Royal Hospital, The
....4 F5

POLICE STATIONS

Albrighton Police Station 29 B3
Bridgnorth Police Station...25 B3
Donnington Police Station....6 G4
Ironbridge Police Station 19 D5
Madeley Police Station 21 C4
Market Drayton Police Station
....28 E3
Newport Police Station 24 F4
Shifnal Police Station 18 H3
Telford Divisional HQ.........16 F1
Wellington Police Station....10 F2

TOURIST INFORMATION CENTRES

Bridgnorth TIC
Tel. 01746 763257 ......25 D3
Ironbridge TIC
Tel. 01952 432166 ......23 A2
Market Drayton TIC
Tel. 01630 653114 ......28 E2
Telford TIC
Tel. 01952 238008 ....1 D4

SCHOOLS & COLLEGES

Abraham Darby School for
Performing Arts 20 H4
Adam's Grammar School ..24 F4
Albrighton Inf. School 29 C3
Albrighton Jun. School...... 29 C3
Apley Wood Prim. School....4 H5
Aqueduct Primary School ..21 A1
Barn Farm Inf. School & Nursery
....10 G4
Blessed Robert Johnson
Catholic College 4 F6
Bridge Special School, The
....21 D1
Bridgnorth Endowed School
....25 D2
Brindleyford Primary School
....21 B1
Brookside Primary School &
Nursery Centre 21 B1
Broseley Prim. School 23 B4
Burton Borough School 24 G4
Captain Webb Primary School
....15 C5
Castle House School 24 F3
Castlefields Primary School
....25 B4
Charlton School 4 E4
Church Aston Inf. School ..24 F6
Cleobury Mortimer Prim. School
....29 B5
Coalbrookdale & Ironbridge
Primary School 19 D5
Dawley Prim. School & Nursery
....15 C4
Donnington Wood Inf. School &
Nursery Centre............ 6 H4
Donnington Wood Jun. School
....6 G5
Dothill Infants School 4 E5
Dothill Junior School..........4 H5
Ercall Junior School, The ..10 G3
Ercall Wood Technology College
....10 F4
Grove School 28 F2
Hadley Infants School........11 A2
Hadley Junior School 11 B1
Hollinswood Infant School &
Nursery.......................16 H2
Hollinswood Jun. School ..16 H2
Holmer Lake Primary School
....21 D1
Idsall School ....18 H
John Fletcher Junior School
....2
John Randall Primary Sch
John Wilkinson Primar
Lacon Childe Schoo

Ladygrove Prim. School 15 C3
Langley St. Leonard's Prim. Sch.
....16 E2
Lawley Primary School 15 A1
Lilleshall Primary School 8 G5
Longlands Prim. School ...28 F2
Lord Silkin School..............16 H5
Madeley Court School 21 B3
Madeley Infants School 21 A5
Madeley Nursery School....21 A3
Malinslee Primary School ..16 E3
Market Drayton Infants School &
Nursery.....................28 E3
Market Drayton Jun. Sch. ..27 D3
Meadows Primary School
....11 C4/C3
Millbrook Primary School ..10 H1
Moorfields Prim. School 24 E5
Mount Gilbert Special School
....10 E1
Muxton Primary School.......7 B3
New College 10 G2
Newdale Prim. School & Nursery
....11 C5
Newport Girls' High School
....24 E5
Newport Infants School 24 G5
Newport Junior School 24 F4
Oakengates Nursery School
....12 E3
Old Hall School.................10 G3
Oldbury Wells School 25 C4
Orleton Park School 9 D1
Phoenix School, The 15 D5
Priorslee Primary School ..13 A5
Queenswood Primary School &
Nursery 1 C1
Randlay Primary School 16 H4
Redhill Primary School 13 B3
Sheriffhales Prim. School ..14 G2
Shifnal Prim. School.........18 H2
Shrewsbury College of Arts &
Technology (Bridgnorth
College Campus).........26 E4
Sir Alexander Fleming Prim. Sch.
....21 C5
Southall Special School 16 E5
St. Andrew's Primary School
....18 H5
St. George's Prim. School 12 H4
St. John's R.C. Primary School
....25 C2
...nard's Inf. School....16 E2
...d's Primary School
....25 C2
...mary School
....6 F5
...hool
A5
21 C4
School
23 C5
29 B5
...5

St. Patrick's R.C. Primary School
....4 E6
St. Peter & St. Paul R.C.
Primary School 24 E3
St. Peter's Primary School ..3 C4
Stirchley Primary School....16 H5
Sutherland School, The 6 F5
Teagues Bridge Primary School
....6 E6
Telford College of Arts &
Technology 10 H2
Thomas Telford School........1 A4
Three Oaks Prim. School ..16 H5
University of Wolverhampton
(Telford Campus) 13 A5
William Reynolds Infants &
Junior Schools............20 H4
Wombridge Prim. School ..12 E3
Woodlands Primary School &
Nursery.....................20 H4
Wrekin College 10 G1
Wrekin View Primary School
....9 D2/10 E1
Wrockwardine Wood
Arts College...............12 F1
Wrockwardine Wood Jun. School
....6 F5
Wrockwardine Wood Inf. School
& Nursery 6 F6

ROUNDABOUTS

Apley Roundabout 4 F6
Beveley Roundabout 11 D3
Birchfield Roundabout 15 B1
Brockton Roundabout........21 D5
Brookside Roundabout 16 H6
Castle Farm Interchange
....13 D6/17 C1
Castlefields Roundabout ..20 H2
Coppice Farm Roundabout
....22 E3
Crow Brook Roundabout 6 E3
Cuckoo Oak Roundabout ..21 D3
Dawley Bank Roundabout 15 D1
Donnington Roundabout......6 H2
Donnington Wood Roundabout
....7 B5
Forge Junction 1 B2
Forge Roundabout 1 C2
Garrison Roundabout 6 G3
Granville Roundabout 6 H6
Greyhound Interchange ...12 F4
Hadley Park Roundabout 5 C4
Halesfield Roundabout 21 D3
Hall Roundabout 1 B3
Heath Hill Roundabout 15 C3
Hollinsgate Roundabout 1 D4
Hollinswood Interchange.....2 F4
Hortonwood Roundabout 6 E4
Jiggers Roundabout
....15 A6/19 D1
Ketley Brook Roundabout..11 A2

Keyley Dingle Interchange 11 B5
Lawley Common Roundabout
....15 B2
Leegomery Roundabout......4 H4
Lees Farm Roundabout 20 H4
Limekiln Bank Roundabout
....13 B3
Madeley Roundabout 21 C4
Malinsee Roundabout.........1 A5
Naird Roundabout.............17 B2
Newdale Roundabout 15 B1
Old Park Roundabout 15 D1
Orchard Farm Roundabout..5 C4
Priorslee Roundabout 2 F1
Randlay Interchange..........17 A3
Shawbury Roundabout 4 E4
St. Georges Roundabout 6 H6
St. Quentins Roundabout ..16 G2
Stirchley Interchange 17 A6
Sutton Hill Roundabout......21 D5
Trench Lock Interchange 5 C6
Wombridge Interchange 12 E1
Woodside Roundabout 21 A3

INDUSTRIAL
ESTATES

Adderley Road Ind. Est. 28 E1
Apley Industrial Area............4 F4
Audley Avenue Business Park
....24 H4
Audley Avenue Industrial Estate
....24 H5
Blockleys Brick Works 11 D1
Bradley Road Ind. Estate 7 A5
Bridges Business Park 15 B4
Buttery Grove Ind. Units 12 F2
Castle Farm Campus 13 C5
Castle Trading Estate 2 F1
Cemetery Road Ind. Area ..15 D1
Central Ordnance Depot......6 E2
Central Park Ind. Area 2 E1
Chartwell Business Park 26 F5
Cockshutt Lane Industrial Area
....23 B3
Court Works Ind. Estate 21 B2
Dawley Bank Ind. Estate ..15 D1
Donnington Wood Business Park
....13 A1
Doseley Ind. Estate 15 B5/B6
Fitchett Industrial Estate....12 G3
Forest Park/Cleobury Ind. Estate
....29 B6
Fort Pendlestone Industrial Area
....26 E1
Gower Street Ind. Estate ..12 G2
Hadley Castle Works 5 C6
Hadley Park Ind. Estate 5 B4
Halesfield Ind. Estate 22 F2
Harcourt Industrial Area 21 D3
Haybridge Ind. Estate 10 H2
Haybrook Ind. Area 22 F3
Heath Hill Ind. Estate 15 B3

Heslop Industrial Area 21 D2
Horsehay Ind. Estate 15 B4
Hortonwood Ind. Estate 5 D4
Ironbridge/Coalbrookdale
Industrial Area 20 E4
Ketley Bank Ind. Estate 11 D4
Ketley Industrial Estate 11 B3
King Street Ind. Estate 23 A4
Knowle Sands Ind. Est. 25 D6
Lightmoor Ind. Area 20 G1
Maer Lane Ind. Estate 28 E1
Maws Craft Centre 22 F5
Orleton Lane Ind. Estate......9 D1
Phoenix Bank Ind. Estate ..28 F3
Priorslee Trading Estate 2 E1
Queensway Campus 5 D5
Railway Sidings Ind. Est. ..18 H3
Redland Ind. Estate 12 G3
Sinclair Industrial Area 11 A3
Old Smithfield Ind. Estate ..18 H3
Snedshill Trading Est. 12 G4
Springfield Ind. Estate.......24 F5
Springfield Retail Area 10 E1
Springhill Trading Estate ..18 H3
St. Georges Road Ind. Est...6 H6
Stafford Park Ind. Estate 2 G3
Stanley Lane Ind.Estate 25 D1
Stanmore Ind. Estate 26 H3
Station Road Ind.Estate 21 B4
Stourbridge Road Ind. Estate
....26 F4
Telford Bridge Retail Park....1 B3
Telford Business Park..........2 E3
Telford Forge Retail Park 1 A2
Telford Science &
Technology Park 17 A3
Telford Shopping Centre 1 C5
Tern Valley Business Park 27 B4
Trench Lock Ind. Estate 5 D6
Tweedale Ind. Estate 21 B2
Walkmill Bridge Business Park
....28 E4
Wellington Retail Park 11 A4
Wrekin Retail Park 11 A4